The PERSEREC report is an excellent academic survey of the available literature on homosexuality in both civilian and military society. Unfortunately, the Bush Administration killed the report because its findings — that homosexuals are qualified for military service — ran afoul of its anti-gay prejudices. When other members of Congress and I asked for an explanation, we were told that the report's mandate was to look at the reliability of homosexuals for security reasons, not the suitability of homosexuals for military service. That's a distinction without a difference. In fact, the report shows that gay men and lesbians are both suitable and reliable for military service. The real question is how long the military can maintain a personnel policy based solely on prejudice.

— *Congresswoman Patricia Schroeder*

★GAYS IN UNIFORM★

The Pentagon's Secret Reports

edited by Kate Dyer

with an introduction by
Congressman Gerry Studds

Boston: Alyson Publications, Inc.

Introduction copyright © 1990 by Gerry Studds.
Foreword copyright © 1990 by Kate Dyer.
Typeset and printed in the United States of America.

This is a trade paperback original from
Alyson Publications, Inc., 40 Plympton Street, Boston, MA 02118.
Distributed in the U.K. by GMP Publishers, P.O. Box 247, London N17 9QR, England.

First edition: September 1990

5 4 3 2

ISBN 1-55583-181-8

Library of Congress Cataloging-in-Publication Data

Gays in uniform : the Pentagon's secret reports / edited by Kate Dyer
; introduction by Gerry S. Studds. — 1st ed.
    p. cm.
Includes bibliographical references.
ISBN 1-55583-181-8 : $6.95
    1. United States—Armed Forces—Gays. 2. United States—Armed
Forces—Recruiting, enlistment, etc. I. Dyer, Kate, 1963- .
UB418.G38G38 1990
355'.008'6642—dc20   90-44672
                                                   CIP

Contents

List of Tables

Introduction

by Congressman Gerry Studds

Each day in my work as a U.S. representative, I face a paper mountain of reports, studies, summaries, outlines, and memoranda for which I have nowhere near enough time. Those written by federal agencies often fall to the bottom of the pile, because verbose "government-ese" tends to weigh a lot and say very little.

On October 17, 1989, however, I was handed a government report that I immediately read from cover to cover. It was a Defense Department study entitled "Nonconforming Sexual Orientations and Military Suitability," and it was a document I had worked for over six months to obtain.

This report — the entirety of which appears in this book — is a scholarly, dispassionate, clear analysis of whether gay men, lesbians, and bisexuals are suitable to serve in the U.S. military. The Defense Department has long maintained that homosexuality is "incompatible with military service," despite the exemplary military records of countless lesbian and gay veterans. Pentagon policy is to automatically reject openly gay applicants and on many occasions it has hunted down and brutally removed those already serving. Its own report, however, seriously questions this policy.

The study's finding is simple and unequivocal: that sexuality "is unrelated to job performance in the same way as is being left- or right-handed." While this conclusion may seem obvious to many, the Department of Defense evidently found it disturbing, and immediately tried to suppress the report.

During five months of calling, writing, and cajoling, my office was told variously that the report was "unavailable," "still under consideration," that it would "be released sometime soon," and on occasion even that "no such report exists." This stonewalling only served to underscore to me the document's importance. Finally, with assistance from House Armed Services Subcommittee Chairwoman Patricia Schroeder, our persistence paid off and the report landed on my desk.

As you will see, it is an extraordinary document. Conceived, financed, and overseen by the Defense Department, it is a refreshingly rational analysis of the ignorance and prejudice that plague gay men and lesbians in the military. It is a compelling, credible study that puts the Pentagon's anti-gay policy in a very dim light indeed.

So dim a light, in fact, that top Pentagon officials fired off rather harshly worded memoranda to their own researchers, chastising them for reaching the conclusions they did. These memoranda also reached us, and provide an instructive glimpse into the behind-the-scenes workings of the Defense Department.

Also included here are the researchers' valiant efforts to explain to their superiors that scientific conclusions "should not be invalidated because they turn out to be problematic from a policy perspective." These memoranda may in many ways prove more extraordinary than the report itself.

Another unanticipated by-product of our struggle came three days after we publicly released the report, when a *second* Pentagon study of homosexuality arrived in an unmarked manila envelope. This second report startlingly suggested that gay men and lesbians display military suitability "that is as good or better than the average heterosexual." I cannot help but wonder how many more Defense Department studies of this nature await our discovery.

These materials — the first report, the internal memoranda, and the second report — are significant historical documents. They effectively debunk the military's baseless contention that gay people are inherently unsuitable for military service. They will no doubt play an important role in ending the shameful discrimination and persecution to which our own military daily subjects an entire class of our citizenry.

This institutionalized prejudice is a national disgrace, and has no place in our armed forces. When it ends — and some day it will — openly gay and lesbian generals, admirals, pilots, and foot soldiers will stand as proud examples of the depth, breadth, and capabilities of our community. These men and women, as visible members of our nation's military, will be on the front lines in the continuing fight to end homophobia, wherever it may be found.

Foreword

Although legendary military leaders such as Alexander the Great and Julius Caesar are widely believed to have been gay, the U.S. military has never accepted its own homosexual members. Ever since George Washington's Continental Army, gay people have been aggressively driven out of the services. At some time viewed as criminal, at others thought to be a mental illness, homosexuality has always been grounds for exclusion or discharge from the American military.

In 1919, the Navy set up a sting operation in Rhode Island, using gay decoy sailors to entice other sailors into sexual liaisons. The Navy then discharged the unwitting sailors for being "perverts," with supporting testimony from the decoy involved.

In 1940, draft board physicians were ordered to screen out suspected homosexuals. A man's lisp or a woman's deep voice could be grounds for immediate disqualification. When World War II created a critical need for more soldiers and sailors, however, these instructions were often ignored by a military desperate for personnel. After the war, veteran gay and lesbian service members were once again persecuted, wartime service notwithstanding. A similar willingness to overlook sexual orientation during Vietnam had no lasting effect — once the conflict was over, so were the careers of any known gay men or lesbians serving.

Gay service members suffered humiliating investigations and ridicule from their colleagues. Friends, family, and acquaintances were often interrogated, destroying personal relationships at a time when they were often most needed. "Confessions" were brutally extracted, and frightened young men and women were brow-beaten into reporting the names of other gay service members. Once dismissed, these soldiers and sailors were identified in discharge papers as homosexual, complicating civilian job-hunting.

Unfortunately, the situation has only worsened. The anti-gay policy's reach was extended significantly during the Reagan Administration, when not only homosexual conduct but mere identification as gay or lesbian became grounds for discipline.

Currently, homosexual status — as opposed to conduct — results in an immediate dismissal. Exceptions to this policy may be made only by the secretary of the affected service. None has ever been granted. Homosexual conduct, on the other hand, if determined by the officer in charge to be an "aberration," and not indicative of the service member's true sexuality, does not automatically result in discharge.

Defense Department policy reads as follows:

> Homosexuality is incompatible with military service. The presence in the military environment of persons who engage in homosexual conduct or who, by their statements, demonstrate a propensity to engage in homosexual conduct, seriously impairs the accomplishment of the military mission. The presence of such members adversely affects the ability of the Military Services to maintain discipline, good order and morale; to foster mutual trust and confidence among service members, to ensure the integrity of rank and command; to facilitate assignment and worldwide deployment of service members who frequently must live and work under close conditions affording minimal privacy; to recruit and retain members of the Military Services; to maintain the public acceptability of military service; and to prevent breaches of security.

Under this policy, no gay person may join the Army, Navy, Air Force, Marines, Coast Guard, or college campus ROTC (Reserve Officer Training Corps) program without lying about his or her sexual orientation. Many do lie in order to serve, and military investigators vigorously seek out and discharge some 2000 service members each year solely because of their sexual orientation. For military women, the numbers are even more alarming: women are three times as likely to be discharged for homosexuality as are their male counterparts.

Each time it discharges someone for this reason, the military squanders the many hours and dollars spent recruiting, training, developing, and supporting that service member. It also robs itself — and the nation — of the many years of service that person would have contributed.

Not surprisingly, the military — though continuing to aggressively enforce it — has a difficult time justifying the policy. For example, the contention that gays somehow patently "impair the accomplishment of the military mission" is unsupported by any scientific analysis. Nor is there any evidence on which to base the assertion that gay service members, by their very presence, "adversely affect good order and morale."

Increasingly, court cases brought by gay and lesbian former soldiers and sailors, and recent campus activism against discrimination in ROTC have forced the military to provide a rationale for its policy. Pentagon spokespersons usually offer a terse "no comment" on this particular issue. Occasionally they elaborate; one spokesman recently explained that "our policy is based on many years of experience and, well, on Defense Department policy."

In an effort to arm itself with more convincing arguments, the Defense Department has conducted studies of the issue on at least three occasions. None of these studies supported its policy.

The first analysis was conducted in 1957 when the secretary of the Navy created a board that was chaired by Captain S. H. Crittenden, Jr., U.S.N. The resulting study, known as the Crittenden Report, examined one of the military's principal justifications for its anti-gay ban: that gays are easy targets for blackmail by enemy agents who might threaten to expose their sexuality. Crittenden, however, concluded that "The number of cases of blackmail as a result of past investigations of homosexuals is negligible. No factual data exist to support the contention that homosexuals are a greater risk than heterosexuals."

Threatened by this finding, the Navy refused to release the report. Twenty years passed and a court order was needed before the study could be pried loose. In the thirty years since Crittenden presented his conclusions, no military studies of the issue had surfaced until the reports contained in this book were released in October 1989.

These 1989 reports resulted from episodes that occurred a few years earlier. In 1987, after the damaging and embarrassing Johnny Walker and Moscow Embassy Marine Guards spy scandals, the Defense Department set up a research facility in Monterey, California, to study personnel security breaches. The resulting Defense Personnel Security Research and Education Center was directed to examine, among other things, homosexuality as "a condition related to trust violation" — the same basic issue Crittenden had answered three decades before.

This time, however, the military researchers did not stop at the question of "reliability" and security secrets. In this study, Dr. Ted Sarbin, a professor of psychology and criminology, and Dr. Ken Karols, a Navy flight surgeon, also examined the more fundamental question of whether homosexuals are "suitable" for service in the Armed Forces.

Their report, "Nonconforming Sexual Orientations and Military Suitability," completed in December 1988 and presented here in its entirety, is a remarkably thoughtful review and analysis of social constructions, legal decisions, and scientific literature regarding homosexuality. It finds unequivocally that gay men and lesbians pose no special security risk and, more importantly, are every bit as suitable for service as heterosexuals.

This conclusion was unacceptable to Pentagon officials, who again attempted to suppress both the report and its findings. They then directed PERSEREC to fundamentally rewrite the report to delete all suggestions that homosexuals could be suitable for service. This process is illustrated in an astonishing series of memoranda between the Defense Department and PERSEREC, included in this book.

Ultimately, U.S. Representatives Gerry Studds of Massachusetts and Patricia Schroeder of Colorado obtained and released the unabridged report. In the substantial media attention that resulted, the Pentagon attempted to discount the report by claiming that PERSEREC was not part of the Defense Department. In fact, PERSEREC was conceived, founded, funded, and administered by the Pentagon and letterhead prominently displays a Department of Defense seal.

Amidst the publicity surrounding the report's release, a second PERSEREC analysis of homosexual suitability — with a similarly damaging conclusion — reached Reps. Studds and Schroeder. This study, conducted by PERSEREC researcher Michael McDaniel, was completed in January 1989, but was never submitted to the Pentagon because of the ongoing antagonism over the Sarbin–Karols report. The complete text of the McDaniel study is also included in this book.

These reports, particularly the Sarbin–Karols work, are important documents. They illuminate the fact that, try as it might, the military is simply unable to justify its anti-gay policy. Sarbin, Karols, and McDaniel were professional researchers commissioned by the Defense Department to examine a significant military issue. None were in any way linked to or invested in the gay and lesbian community. None had any "axe to grind" regarding the military or the policy. Indeed, any bias they might have had would most likely have been toward existing military policy.

These reports — from within the military itself — play a crucial role in the fight to reverse the policy. National organizations such as the American Civil Liberties Union, the American Psychological Association, the National Organization for Women, Citizen Soldier, the Central Committee for Conscientious Objectors, the Midwest

Committee for Military Counseling, and the National Lawyers Guild have joined may gay and lesbian groups in this fight.

Through lobbying, litigation, and campus activism against the ROTC discrimination, these and other groups hope to tear down this last bastion of institutionalized homophobia. The military is, after all, the country's largest single employer. Its history, traditions, and values pervade our culture. Long regarded as a rite of passage, military service has been the first step in many a successful career path. Yet, acting under its own set of regulations and immune from state and municipal laws that forbid discrimination based on sexual orientation, this cultural and political giant remains closed — at least officially — to gay men and lesbians.

Before President Truman ordered the Armed Forces desegregated in 1948, they were similarly closed to African-Americans. Using precisely the same arguments heard today with regard to gay people, the military stubbornly resisted desegregation. Pentagon officials claimed that Truman's order would "seriously impair the accomplishment of the military mission," and that "no white man will ever take an order from a black man." Forty years later, every man and woman in uniform is taking orders from a black chairman of the Joint Chiefs of Staff.

Without a doubt, many are also unwittingly taking orders from gay men and lesbians as well. Until the policy is reversed, however, those gay people issuing orders, as well as those faithfully carrying them out, are not welcome in our military. These two military studies present a compelling argument that they should be.

Part 1: The First Report

Nonconforming Sexual Orientations and Military Suitability

Nonconforming Sexual Orientations
and Military Suitability

Prepared by
Theodore R. Sarbin, Ph.D.
and
Kenneth E. Karols, M.D., Ph.D.

Released by
Carson K. Eoyang, Director

Defense Personnel Security Research and Education Center

Preface

The Defense Personnel Security Research and Education Center (PERSEREC) performs research and analyses in support of DoD's personnel security programs. One of its top priority projects approved by OSD is to validate existing criteria for personnel security clearance determinations and to develop more objective, uniform, and valid adjudication standards, e.g., clarify relationships between risk and various personal characteristics.

In exploring the range of antecedent conditions related to trust violation, PERSEREC is examining such factors as drug and alcohol abuse, credit history, psychiatric disorders, and nonconforming sexual behaviors. In this context, a comprehensive review of the scientific literature on homosexuality was undertaken to illuminate the relationship between homosexuality and security. It quickly became apparent that security risk per se is also related to a larger problem; namely, the suitability of homosexuals for military service. This report provides a historical review of the various social constructions that have been placed on homosexuality, the effects of legal decisions and changing folkways, and a summary of the scientific literature. Current employment practices within DoD are reviewed in the light of conclusions drawn from this study.

This study was initiated to obtain the broadest range of scientific input in the formulation and revision of agency policy. No single study, either formally sponsored or not, is necessarily reflective of current or future policy; each is considered on its merits in the entire context of the social, legal, scientific, military, and political ramifications as it may affect national security. Finally, the knowledge and insight derived from an accumulation of rigorous studies and analyses will contribute to the development of appropriate policy.

Carson K. Eoyang
Director, PERSEREC

i

Nonconforming Sexual Orientations
and Military Suitability

Theodore R. Sarbin, Ph.D.
and
Kenneth E. Karols, M.D., Ph.D.

Summary

Background and Issue

This study of the suitability of homosexuals for military service was prepared in the context of our continuing search for connections between personal history items and the potential for security violations. If homosexuality is unrelated to job performance (including the observance of security regulations), then the central issue is the validity of DoD's long-time practice of denying military employment to homosexuals solely on the basis of their sexual orientation.

Objectives

The research objective was to write a paper that reviews (1) changing folkways and court decisions, (2) the current scientific status of atypical sexual orientation, and (3) the history of changing social constructions of nonconforming sexual behavior. These reviews provide the background for an examination of current personnel practices.

Approach

From current scientific publications, legal studies, and social science literature, we abstracted findings pertinent to the issue of whether homosexuals are suitable for military service, and by extension, suitable for security clearance. The authors bring to the task different but overlapping frameworks: social psychology and forensic psychiatry.

Results

The product of our efforts is a scholarly document that examines public attitudes, recent legal decisions, and the findings from biological science. The development of

ii

ethnology has made possible more precise studies of the influence of biological factors on the formation of sexual orientation. In addition to data supporting a biological factor in the causal nexus, we have examined recent and contemporary studies that lead to the inference that homosexual men and women as a group are not different from heterosexual men and women in regard to adjustment criteria or job performance. An important feature of our report is a historical analysis of four distinct constructions placed on homosexual conduct: sin, crime, sickness, and minority group behavior.

Conclusions/Recommendations

We conclude that the time is ripe for engaging in empirical research to test the hypothesis that men and women of atypical sexual orientation can function appropriately in military units. We suggest a general framework for developing research programs. The findings from such research could be employed by policy makers as they continue their efforts to improve the effectiveness of recruitment, selection, and training programs.

iii

Introduction

Given continuing manpower needs in the armed forces and also social pressures to remove traditional barriers that exclude homosexual men and women from military service, it is timely to review current perspectives on homosexuality. As context for this review, we examine three kinds of relevant information: (1) judicial trends and shifting folkways, (2) contemporary scientific contributions, and (3) historical and current social constructions of homosexuality.

Inferences drawn from these formulations will serve as a background for examining the currency of existing military codes and for considering the potential outcomes of maintaining or modifying these codes.

It is a common practice to employ the concept of sexual preference in discussions of same-gender and opposite-gender issues. The use of "preference" is misleading except for persons who are bisexual, that is, those to whom either gender is acceptable as a sex partner. For most other cases, the gender choice of sex partner is not a matter of "preference." The desired gender of the sex partner is fixed or at least firmly conditioned by biological preparation and habits laid down early in life. Embryological events and the subsequent reinforcement history of gender-related acts create a condition that might better be labeled sexual **orientation** or sexual **status**.

1

Judicial Trends and Shifting Folkways

It is beyond the scope of this paper to review in detail the numerous decisions handed down by the courts in recent years that demonstrate the effects of social movements dedicated to advancing civil rights (Barnett, 1973). Such decisions, together with legislative acts in various jurisdictions, have signalled a breakthrough in the conceptual reconstruction of persons whose sexual orientations are nonconforming to majority custom and expectations. A celebrated case was that of Norton v. Macy (1969). The plaintiff had been fired on the grounds of immorality because he had engaged in homosexual conduct. The court ruled that alleged or proven immoral conduct is not grounds for separation from public employment unless it can be shown that such behavior has demonstrable effects on job performance. Judge David Bazelon's decision included a statement that has softened discriminatory employment practices, and may have influenced more recent decisions affecting personnel in the military services. He said (in part):

> The notion that it could be an appropriate function of the federal bureaucracy to enforce the majority's conventional codes of conduct in the private lives of its employees is at war with elementary concepts of liberty, privacy, and diversity (1969).

Other judicial decisions since Norton have propelled society to acknowledge that discriminatory practices toward homosexuals are not consonant with constitutional guarantees of individual autonomy and equal protection. A case that drew national media attention in 1975 is that of Sergeant Leonard P. Matlovich ("Homosexual Sergeant", 1975). Matlovich was dismissed from the Air Force with a less than honorable discharge after he voluntarily admitted that he was a homosexual. A 12-year veteran who served in combat in Vietnam, he had been awarded Bronze Star and Purple Heart medals and had an exemplary performance record up to the time he was dismissed. The bases for his separation from military service were the codified Department of Defense and Air Force regulations that persons who admitted to homosexual orientation or conduct could not serve in the Air Force. In 1978, the United States Court of Appeals in Washington, DC, ruled that the Air Force had acted improperly in discharging Sergeant Matlovich without specifying appropriate reasons other than being homosexual. In 1981, the same court awarded him back pay and a retroactive promotion (Guevarra, 1988).

The more recent case of Sergeant Perry Watkins (Henry, 1988) may have profound implications for future legal challenges. Watkins entered the service in 1967 at age 19, admitting on a preinduction medical form that he had homosexual tendencies. At that time, the Army discharged soldiers for engaging in homosexual acts, but not for "homosexuality." The distinction between homosexual acts and homosexuality is difficult to draw. The authors of the regulation probably employed a notion that was

3

influenced by the dichotomy: acts and dispositions. The abstract term, "homosexuality," could be employed to denote that a person might be disposed to act in certain ways, but would not necessarily engage in such overt actions.

In 1981, the regulation was modified to include sexual orientation, regardless of conduct. On the basis of this regulation, Watkins was dismissed from the service in 1984 after a series of court actions. In February, 1988, a three-judge panel of the United States Court of Appeals for the Ninth Circuit ruled two to one that the Army's discrimination against homosexuals was unconstitutional. The Court held that the regulation violated the constitutional guarantee of equal rights under the law. The language of the court compared discrimination against homosexuals with racial discrimination. Writing the majority opinion, Judge William Norris included the following analogy:

> For much of our history, the military's fear of racial tension kept black soldiers separated from whites. Today it is unthinkable that the judiciary would defer to the Army's prior 'professional' judgment that black and white soldiers had to be segregated to avoid interracial tensions.

Three months after rendering its decision, the same court granted the Army's petition for a rehearing (Bishop, 1988). As of this writing (October 1988), the rehearing is being conducted in San Francisco before a panel of 11 judges (Egelko, 1988).

Besides judicial rulings that impinge directly on the right of homosexuals to employment in the military services, a number of court decisions have provided additional context for examining discrimination in civilian employment. One of the more recent cases was tried in the Federal District Court in San Francisco in 1987. The case was filed in 1984 on behalf of an organization of Silicon Valley (California) workers known as High Tech Gays. Three members of this group brought the suit after they had been denied security clearances because of the policy of intensive and extensive scrutiny of homosexuals. Identification of a prospective employee as homosexual was sufficient reason, according to Department of Defense policies, for expanded and intensive clearance investigations. The ruling handed down by Judge Thelton E. Henderson declared that the policies of the Department of Defense were founded on prejudice and stereotypes, the basis for the policy being the unwarranted claim that homosexual men and women were emotionally unstable and, therefore, candidates for blackmail. Judge Henderson ruled that the policies violated the guarantee of equal protection under the law. If upheld by higher courts, the equal protection guarantee would eliminate sexual orientation as a basis for differential background investigations when a man or woman applies for security clearance in the private sector (High Tech Gays v. Defense Industrial Security Clearance Office, 1987). A stay on this order has been granted since the matter is under judicial review.

4

Since law and custom tend to influence each other, it is instructive to note shifts in social practice in dealing with discrimination against homosexuals. In 1977, the U.S. Commission on Civil Rights took jurisdiction of cases in which discrimination on the basis of sexual orientation had been alleged, such as police harassment of homosexual men and women (1977). The Civil Service Commission in 1975 and 1976 amended its regulations so that no person would be denied Federal employment on the basis of sexual orientation (see Singer v. Civil Service Commission, 1975, 1977). The National Security Agency has recently moved to grant homosexuals sensitive compartmented information (SCI) security clearances (Rosa, 1988), one of the highest classifications for access to sensitive information. In June 1988, the Veterans Administration (VA) modified its rules with regard to benefits for veterans discharged for homosexuality. Those discharged prior to 1980 had as a rule been given a less than honorable discharge characterization which resulted in denial of most benefits. The VA has now upgraded those discharges. "The new rule was proposed as a matter of fairness" (Maze, 1988).

In 1978, it was reported that nearly a quarter of America's largest corporations on the Fortune 500 list had instituted policies to guarantee equal opportunity to homosexual employees (Vetri, 1980). Another sign of the changing folkways is the granting of recognition to political groups supporting equal rights for homosexuals (Vetri, 1980). Many universities have adopted nondiscriminatory policies in hiring, housing, and opportunities for advancement. Municipalities by the score have adopted nondiscrimination ordinances. In the State of California, municipalities and counties are no longer using the category of sexual orientation in the hiring of police officers. This appears to be the outcome of the current legal and social climate. Sexual orientation is not (in California at least) considered a legitimate BFOQ (bonafide occupational qualification) and few, if any, employers are willing to risk legal challenge by discriminating against homosexuals. Although there is no specific State legislation in California prohibiting employment discrimination on the basis of sexual orientation, discrimination based on sexual orientation in services is prohibited by the Unruh Civil Rights Act, and in other areas by Civil Code sections 51.7, 52 and 52.1, as well as by Penal Code section 422.6-422.9 and 1170.75. California Attorney General Van de Kamp has also interpreted the labor code as protecting homosexuals from discrimination.

A recent Supreme Court decision, which addressed another aspect of the rights of persons who hold nonconforming sexual orientations, may be seen as a further indicator of change. In Webster v. Doe, (1988), the Court held that it is legitimate for courts to review the constitutionality of the CIA's dismissal of employees. In 1982, "John Doe," described as a covert electronics technician, voluntarily told an Agency security officer that he was a homosexual. The Agency conducted a thorough investigation, including a polygraph examination designed to uncover whether he had disclosed classified information. Although Doe passed the test, he was dismissed by then director William J. Casey on the grounds that he was a national security risk. The effect of this Supreme Court decision is that Doe can now appeal to the Federal courts to sustain

5

his argument that his constitutional rights had been violated because there was no evidence that he could not be trusted with national security secrets (Stuart, 1988).

To be sure, traditional attitudes are resistant to change. Not all legal rulings and social practices are favorable to policies supporting nondiscrimination on the basis of sexual orientation. Nonetheless, the instances cited above are more than straws in the wind. One interpretation to place on these judicial decisions is that folkways are shifting from intolerance to indifference, if not to open-hearted tolerance. This shift in folkways is reflected, in part, in the repeal of vaguely written and differentially enforced sodomy statutes in nearly half the States, thus decriminalizing homosexual conduct (not to mention decriminalizing unconventional but widely practiced forms of heterosexual conduct). In this connection, it is instructive to refer to a study conducted by Geis and associates (1976) to throw some light on the claim that decriminalization of sodomy between consenting adults would increase the incidence of sex crimes. A survey was conducted in seven States that had decriminalized private homosexual behavior between consenting adults. Decriminalization appeared not to have increased the number of sex crimes nor the amount of private homosexual conduct.

6

Scientific Status of the Homosexuality Concept

For nearly a century, sexuality has been an object of intensive scientific study. In the past two decades, with the advent of advances in biotechnology, psychology, ethnology, and methods of social analysis, numerous systematic researches have yielded findings relevant to the formulation of law and public policy.

The emergence of scientific medicine in the nineteenth century brought with it the practice of assigning medical causes to conduct that had earlier been construed as sin or crime. In this context, scientific theories were formulated to explain homosexual behavior in terms of heredity and degenerative disease of the central nervous system. The pioneers in the scientific study of sexuality, Richard von Kraft-Ebing (1880/1922) and Havelock Ellis (1915) argued that homosexuality was an inborn condition. An alternate view was advanced by Sigmund Freud (1905/1938) and other psychoanalytic writers who traced the cause of homosexual conduct to faulty psychosocial development resulting in an arrest or a fixation at an early stage. The power structure of the family, typically a dominant but seductive mother and a weak father, was offered as the major cause of nonconforming sexual orientation. Thus, from the beginnings of scientific inquiry, theories of sexuality reflected different emphases: biological vs. psychosocial, or nature vs. nurture. Contemporary theories reflect these contrary orientations (Kolodny, Masters, and Johnson, 1979).

In the 1920s, with advances in endocrinology and biochemistry, new theories appeared that related sexual behavior to levels of sex hormones. Little solid evidence has been presented, however, to support a hypothesized link between homosexual conduct and circulating hormone levels in adults.

Advances in methodology stimulated a renewed interest in genetic research. The study of twins has been a fruitful source of genetic hypotheses. Kallman (1952) reported a concordance rate of 100 percent for "homosexuality" for 40 pairs of identical twins. That is, when one of a pair of identical twins was identified as homosexual, the other was also found to be homosexual. This occurred even when the twins had been raised apart. The author of the study cautioned that the data are not conclusive in supporting the genetic hypothesis--the twins may have responded to the same socializing influences. In this connection, Marmor (1975), a well-known psychiatrist, claimed that the "most prevalent theory concerning the cause of homosexuality is that which attributes it to a pathogenic family background."

Perhaps the most thorough research undertaken to advance the frontiers of knowledge about sexuality was that of Alfred Kinsey (Kinsey, Pomeroy, & Martin, 1948; Kinsey, Pomeroy, Martin, & Gebhard, 1953). A zoologist, Kinsey organized his research program along ethological and epidemiological lines. The variable of interest for Kinsey was sexual acts. The raw data for his studies were obtained through structured

7

intensive interviews. In contemporary scientific fashion, quantitative analysis guided his work and influenced his conclusions. He employed a rating scale that allowed him to rate subjects from 0 to 6. (A category "x" was used to identify persons with no "socio-sexual" response, mostly young children.) From the interview data, he compiled ratings on the hetero-homosexual dimension for a large sample of respondents. The rating of 0 was assigned to men who were exclusively heterosexual, and 6 to men who were exclusively homosexual. The rating 1 was assigned to men who were predominantly heterosexual, and 5 to men who were predominantly homosexual, and so on. (The Kinsey scale is reproduced in Appendix C.)

Kinsey reported many significant findings, among them that 50 percent of the white male population were exclusively heterosexual and 4 percent were exclusively homosexual throughout adult life. Forty-six percent had some homosexual experience throughout adult life. Between the ages of 16 and 65, 10 percent of the men met Kinsey's criterion of "more or less exclusively homosexual."

In the fashion of ethological research, Kinsey was primarily concerned with presenting prevalence statistics. Whether the dimension was based on nature or nurture, or a combination of these, was not an important concern.

During the past 30 years, increasing knowledge in molecular biology, endocrinology, embryology, and developmental neurology has made it possible to state with confidence that male and female brains are structurally different in certain areas concerned with glandular and sexual functions, especially in the hypothalamus and related subcortical systems (Kelly, 1985). The actions of the various sex hormones in the differentiation of male and female anatomy have been charted. Developmentally, there is a built-in bias toward differentiating an organism into a female, i.e., "nature makes females." On the basis of extensive research, Money and Erhardt (1972) concluded: "...in the total absence of male gonadal [sex] hormones, the fetus always continues to differentiate the reproductive anatomy of the female." This process takes place regardless of the basic masculinity (XY chromosomes) or femininity (XX chromosomes) of the fetus. The bias is counteracted approximately 50 percent of the time by the action of male hormones. The discovery of this built-in mechanism toward femaleness sparked additional research that ultimately illuminated the phenomenon of same-gender attraction. It has been recognized for some time that parts of the brain are glandular and secrete neurohormonal substances that have far-reaching effects. Not unlike the better-known sex hormones, the androgens and estrogens, these brain neurohormonal substances also appear to have profound effects on development.

From a review of ethnographic reports, historical sources, biographies, and literary works, it is apparent that some same-gender orientation is universally observed (Bullough, 1976; Howells, 1984; Marshall & Suggs, 1971). The world-wide prevalence of exclusive same-gender orientation is estimated as three to five percent in the male

8

population, regardless of social tolerance, as in the Philippines, Polynesia and Brazil, intolerance as in the United States, or repression as in the Soviet Union (Mihalek, 1988). This constancy in the face of cultural diversity suggests that biological factors may be the fundamental source of homosexual orientation.

From these observations, as well as intensive analysis of more than 300 research reports, Ellis and Ames (1987) have advanced a multi-factorial theory of sexuality, including same-gender attraction. They conclude that current scientific findings support the view that hormonal and neurological variables operating during the gestation period are the main contributors to sexual orientation. For the ultimate formation of sexual identity, the Ellis-Ames theory does not exclude psychosocial experience as a potential modifier of the phenotypical expression of biological development.

From their review of current research, Ellis and Ames propose that sexuality be studied through the consideration of five dimensions. These are: genetic (the effects of sex chromosomes, XX and XY, and various anomalous karyotypes); genital (effects of internal and external genitalia, the male-female differentiation, which begins in the first month of embryonic life); nongenital morphological (effects of secondary sex characteristics--body build, voice, hair distribution); neurological (male and female brain differentiation and associated sex-typical actions--social influences and the formation of sex-typed roles). Most of the events shaping the developing organism's sexuality along these dimensions occur between the first and fifth months of intrauterine life. These events are controlled by the interaction of delicate balances between the various male and female hormones and their associated enzyme systems. Development of the embryo can be influenced by several factors affecting the internal environment of the mother, such as genetic hormonal background, pharmacological influences and immunological conditions, not to mention the psychophysiological effects arising from the social environment. Disturbances in any one or any combination of these factors can result in alterations in sexual development called inversions. These inversions are failures of the embryo to differentiate fully in any of the other sexual dimensions (genital, morphological, neurological, or behavioral) according to chromosomal patterns. These anomalies of embryonic development are central to the later development of sexual orientation and behavior such as same-sex attraction, bisexuality, and other nonconforming patterns. As support for their theory, Ellis and Ames cite various experiments with animals in which permanent changes in sexual behavior have been induced by glandular and other treatments. The changes noted in these experimental animals are similar to those in humans with known anomalies of endocrine and enzyme systems.

Adult sexual orientation, then, has its origins, if not its expression, in embryonic development. Ellis and Ames conclude that:

9

complex combinations of genetic, hormonal, neurological, and environmental factors operating prior to birth largely determines what an individual's sexual orientation will be, although the orientation itself awaits the onset of puberty to be activated, and may not entirely stabilize until early adulthood (p. 251).

The conclusions are consistent with those of John Money (1988), a leading researcher on the psychobiology of sex. According to Money, in his recent review and summary of current knowledge on homosexuality, data from clinical and laboratory sources indicate that:

> in all species, the differentiation of sexual orientation or status as either bisexual or monosexual (i.e., exclusively heterosexual or homosexual) is a sequential process. The prenatal state of this process, with a possible brief neonatal extension, takes place under the aegis of brain hormonalization. It continues postnatally under the aegis of the senses and social communication of learning (p.49).

Our brief overview of scientific findings instructs us that the phenomena that we label sexuality are complex, and that we must assign credibility to the notion that overt and fantasy expressions of sexuality are influenced by multiple antecedents. The leading authorities agree that these expressions are best described in terms of gradations or dimensions, rather than by the rigidly-bound, mutually exclusive categories, "heterosexual" and "homosexual." Of special importance is the recognition of the interplay of biological and social factors.

10

The Social Construction of Sexual Deviance

The foregoing account summarizes the current scientific knowledge about sexual orientation and conduct. The most obvious conclusion emerging from this review is <u>variability</u> in sexual orientation, role, identity, life style, and conduct. The recognition of such variability dictates that we construct our beliefs and our policies on the recognition of gradations of continuous dimensions, rather than on the notion of discrete categories. To use an overworked metaphor, black and white are anchoring points for an achromatic color dimension, and between these anchoring points are innumerable shades of grey. Other dimensions come into play when considering chromatic stimuli, such as hue, saturation, brightness and texture. Similarly, the multidimensional concept of sexuality is contrary to the assertions of earlier generations of theologians, moralists, and politicians whose construal of sexuality was achieved under the guidance of two-valued logic in which narrowly defined heterosexual orientation and conduct were assigned to the category, "normal," and any departures from the customary were assigned to the category, "abnormal."

We have already alluded to the research of Alfred Kinsey (1948, 1953), a turning point in the history of the social construction of sexuality. After detailed analysis of the sexual histories of thousands of people, Kinsey (1948) concluded that the class "human beings" does not represent two discrete populations, heterosexual and homosexual, and that the world:

> is not to be divided into sheep and goats....It is a fundamental of taxonomy that nature rarely deals with discrete categories. Only the human mind invents categories and tries to force facts into separate pigeonholes. The living world is a continuum in each and every one of its aspects. The sooner we learn this concerning human sexual behavior the sooner we shall reach a sound understanding of the realities of sex (p. 639).

The observations of historians (see, for example, Bullough, 1976) and the reports of ethnographers (see, for example, Ford and Beach, 1951; Marshall & Suggs, 1971; and Devereaux, 1963) support the notion that the constructions placed on same-gender sexuality are social. As Kinsey remarked, "only the human mind invents categories." At certain times, and in many societies, most variations in the expression of sexuality have been regarded as normal. It is the application of moral rules and legal statutes that determines whether same-gender orientation and conduct is classified as acceptable, tolerable, offensive, or criminal. Such rules and statutes are the products of custom, supported by the power vested in authority. As the historical record shows with abundant clarity, forms of authority change. In early times, moral rules were enforced by men and women enacting priestly roles. Later, ruling classes imposed

11

their own fluctuating standards on the enforcement of moral rules. In modern times, rules are constructed through consensus or legislation, and in the case of democracies, rules favoring the majority are tempered so that rights of minorities are not obliterated.

How has this variability been construed? Tracing the history of social constructions of deviant conduct points unmistakably to the influence of concurrent belief systems. A full historical account is beyond the scope of this paper, but for our purposes, it is sufficient to demonstrate that observed variability in sexual conduct has been construed differently at different times in Western history. Our point of departure is a contemporary one: that observations ("facts") are raw materials for constructing meanings (Spector & Kitsuse, 1987). The construction of meanings is not given in the observations, but is the product of cognitive work, taking into account political, social and religious contexts. In the past several hundred years, four constructions have been offered to account for variations in sexual orientation. Evidence of these constructions is abundant in contemporary life, although each construction was initially formulated in a different historical period.

The Morality Construction--Good and Evil as Fundamental Categories.

Judeo-Christian moral rules as represented in the Bible are the source of the long-held construction of prohibition of nonprocreative sexual conduct. Masturbation, lascivious conduct, and nonprocreative sex were proscribed. "You shall not lie with a man as with a woman, that is an abomination" (Leviticus 18:22). "Neither the immoral, nor idolaters, nor adulterers, nor abusers of themselves with mankind, will inherit the Kingdom of God" (I Corinthians 6:9).

The history of religious attempts to control sex makes clear the notion of variability in attitudes. Struggles between advocates of different theological doctrines have been reflected in attitudes toward sex. In the formation of attitudes, two ideas stand out; first, the inferior status of women, and, second, child-bearing as a requirement for maintaining a collectivity. In a penetrating review, Law (1988) provides evidence and argument to support the proposition that the condemnation of homosexuality is more an unwitting reaction to the violation of traditional gender norms than to nonconforming sexual practices. When a man adopts the female role in a sexual relationship, he gives up his masculinity for the inferiority that is associated with being a woman. This constituted, for some Church authorities, an abomination, a sin against nature (Bullough 1976). Except for the occasional advocacy of celibacy,* early doctrine

---

*It is curious that so many religious thinkers have held celibacy as the highest moral goal. Celibacy, especially if lifelong, as practiced by priests, monks and nuns, denies not only sexual behavior but the sexual impulse itself. If one accepts the logic behind

12

held that sex served only one purpose: procreation. This doctrine was supported by the claim that such was God's intention in creating the world of nature. Therefore, sex for pleasure was suspect, especially same-gender sex, since this is obviously non-procreational. The appellation, "sins against nature," appears frequently in doctrinal arguments (Bullough, 1976). Since same-gender sex was nonprocreative, it clearly was a sin against nature.

In the Judeo-Christian traditions, Good and Evil are the categories that provide the background for declaring value judgments on sexual nonconformity. Arising from primitive taboos, the powerful image of "sin" was employed to define the unwanted conduct. Fundamentalist preachers who take the Scriptures as the literal revealed Word of God are contemporary advocates of the belief that nonconforming sexual behavior is sinful. The attribution of sinfulness carries multiple meanings: among some groups, sin is explained as voluntary acceptance of Satanic influence; among others sin is believed to produce a flawed or spoiled identity. Societal reactions to sin include ostracism, corporal punishment, imprisonment and in more draconian times, torture, stoning, hanging, burning at the stake, and even genocide.

Sin is an attribution, a construction made by others or by oneself. Its force lies in its attachment to entrenched religious doctrine. Like taboos, the concept of sin is acquired by people before they reach the age of reflection. The argument that sin is a social construction is nowhere better illustrated than in the debates of theologians who have puzzled over the criteria for sinful conduct: under what conditions should an action be regarded as a venial sin or as a mortal sin?

The Legal Construction--Sexual Deviance as Criminal Behavior.

Arising from religious precepts, legislative acts were introduced to control nonprocreative sexual behavior. Ruse (1988), commenting on the relationship of laws designed to control sexual behavior to Judeo-Christian religious teachings says:

> the very terms used for anal intercourse show their origins
> in a philosophy which intertwines law and Judaeo-Christian
> morality. "Sodomy" obviously comes from the name of the
> doomed city of the plain, and "buggery" is a corruption of
> "bougrerie," named after so-called "Bulgarian" heretics who
> were guilty of a form of Manichean heresy, Albigensianism.
> They believed that physical things are evil, and thus refused

---

the banning of nonprocreational sex acts, life-long celibacy would have to be construed as "unnatural" and therefore sinful behavior.

13

to propagate the species, turning therefore to other sexual outlets. Hence banning buggery struck a two-fold blow for morality: against unnatural vice and against heretical religion (p. 246).

As early as 1533 in England, buggery, which had been established in religion as a sin against nature, was declared a crime. In the ensuing three decades, the statute was repealed and reenacted several times. In 1563, in the reign of Elizabeth I, the law against buggery became firmly established. Criminal codes provided severe punishment for persons accused of nonconforming sexual conduct (Bullough, 1976). The language of such statutes is not uniform. Buggery, sodomy, lewdness, perversion, lasciviousness, and even immorality are terms that have been employed in different statutes and at various times to denote the proscribed criminal conduct.

The underlying categories of the legal construction of nonconforming sexuality are continuous with those of the religious construction: good and evil. With the secularization of morality, sin was no longer an appropriate descriptor for unwanted conduct. The transition from "sins against nature" to "crimes against nature" was an accomplishment of the secularization and attempted legalization of morality. Crime, the secular equivalent of sin, became the preferred descriptive term.

To make rational the use of the crime concept in the context of sexual behavior, it had to be consonant with accepted legal usage, as in crimes against the person, crimes against property, crimes against the Crown, etc. The linguistic formula "crimes against..." presupposes a victim. In following this logic, early practitioners of jurisprudence created "crimes against nature" as the label for unwanted sexual conduct. In so doing, they implied that "nature" was the victim.

In most of the criminal codes, and in the Uniform Code of Military Justice, the concept of "crimes against nature" appears frequently when sexual behavior is proscribed. The concept is sometimes rendered by the employment of language which includes the adjective, "unnatural." Clearly, the authors of statutes that proscribe "crimes against nature" were not using "nature" as a descriptor for flora and fauna, mountains and valleys, oceans and deserts. When "nature" is the victim, something else is intended.

The statutory language, as we mentioned before, is derived from the religious idiom, "sins against nature." "Nature" is employed in the sense used by the early Greek philosophers, as the force or essence that resides within things. Thus, it is in the nature of a hen's egg to develop into a chicken, for water to run downhill, etc. This concept of nature served as the main explanatory principle, employed as an all-purpose answer for "why" questions. With the development of empirical science, "why" questions became superfluous, they gave way to "how" questions, and answers were formulated

14

according to laws and principles constructed through observation and experiment. At the present time, the legal concept, "crimes against nature," is defensible only as a rhetorical device to control nonprocreative sex. It has no scientific status.*

The Sickness Construction--The Medicalization of Deviance

The nineteenth century witnessed the social construction of deviant conduct as sickness. Although the medical model of deviance had its origins in the sixteenth century, it was not until the growth and success of technology and science in the nineteenth century that medical practitioners created elaborate theories to account for unwanted conduct. Many of the fanciful early theories of crime and craziness were given credibility because they were uttered by physicians and, therefore, presumed to be scientific. The prestige conferred upon the practitioners of science and technology blanketed the medical profession. It was during the latter half of the century that medical scientists initiated the movement to "medicalize" not only poorly understood somatic dysfunctions, but all human behavior. Conduct that in the past had been assigned to moralists or to the law now came under the purview of medical authority. Deviant conduct of any kind became topics of interest for doctors. The brain had already been given its place as the most important coordinating organ of the body, and the "mind" was somehow located in the brain. Therefore, any item of behavior that was nonconformant with current norms could be attributed to faulty brain apparatus, flawed mental structures, or both. In the absence of robust psychological theories, the observation and study of nonconforming behavior led physicians to assimilate theories of social misconduct to theories of somatic disease. The creation and elaboration of disease theories was based upon the all-encompassing notion that every human action could be accounted for through the application of the laws of chemistry and physics. In this context, homosexuality and other nonprocreative forms of sexual conduct were construed as sickness. To be sure, the medicalization of nonconforming sexual conduct failed to replace entirely the older moral and criminal constructions, and in many cases persons suffering from such illnesses continued to be punished.

It is interesting to note that the term, "homosexuality," itself did not appear in English writings until the 1890s. Like most medical terms, it was created out of Greek and Latin roots. Prior to that time, labels for nonconforming sexual conduct in the English language had been free of medical connotations, as, for example, the words sodomy, buggery, perversion, corruption, lewdness, and wantonness. One outcome of the medicalization of nonconforming sexual conduct was the inclusion of homosexuality in textbooks of psychiatry and medical psychology. Homosexuality was officially listed

---

*This is not to gainsay the use of this metaphor to connote such events as nuclear war and the pollution of our atmosphere and our rivers, lakes and oceans.

15

as an illness in the 1933 precursor to the 1952 Diagnostic and Statistical Manual of the American Psychiatric Association (DSM-I). In the 1930s and 1940s any person who admitted being homosexual was likely to be referred to a psychiatrist for diagnosis and treatment--the goal of the treatment being the elimination of the homosexual interest. But even during this period the father of psychoanalysis, Freud, expressed the opinion that homosexuality was not an illness. In 1935 Freud wrote a letter to the troubled mother of a homsexual which is worth quoting in its entirety (Bieber et al., 1962), as it anticipates and eloquently summarizes the prevailing current scientific and medical views on homosexuality.

April 9, 1935

Dear Mrs. ____

I gather from your letter that your son is a homosexual. . . . Homosexuality is assuredly no advantage, but it is nothing to be ashamed of, no vice, no degradation, it cannot be classified as an illness; we consider it to be a variation of the sexual function produced by a certain arrest of sexual development. . . By asking me if I can help, you mean, I suppose, if I can abolish homsexuality and make normal heterosexuality take its place. The answer is, in a general way, we cannot promise to achieve it. In a certain number of cases we succeed in developing the blighted germs of heterosexual tendencies which are present in every homosexual, in the majority of cases it is no more possible. It is a question of the quality and the age of the individual. The result of treatment cannot be predicted.

What analysis can do for your son runs in a different line. If he is unhappy, neurotic, torn by conflicts, inhibited in his social life, analysis may bring him harmony, peace of mind, full efficiency, whether he remains a homosexual or gets changed. . .

Sincerely yours with kind wishes,

Freud

Homosexuality as a social construction is nowhere better illustrated than in the arbitrary manner in which it was included and ultimately excluded from the medical lexicon. In 1974, the diagnosis of homosexuality was deleted from the Diagnostic Manual of the American Psychiatric Association under pressure from many psychiatrists who argued that homosexuality was more correctly construed as a nonconforming life style rather than as a mental disease. This was essentially a political decision, taken by majority vote of the Association.

Although the mental health professions do not speak with one voice, the currently prevailing view was advanced by Marmor (Freedman, Kaplan & Sadock, 1975), at that time president of the American Psychiatric Association: "...there is no reason to assume that there is a specific psychodynamic structure to homosexuality anymore than there is to heterosexuality" (p. 1514). The American Psychological Association passed a resolution in 1975 declaring that:

16

homosexuality per se implies no impairment in judgment, stability, reliability or general social or vocational capabilities. ...The Association deplores all public and private discrimination in such areas as employment, housing, public accommodation, and licensing....The Association supports and urges the enactment of civil rights legislation...that would offer citizens who engage in homosexuality the same protections now guaranteed to others on the basis of race, creed, color, etc.

Substantially the same resolution was enacted by the American Psychiatric Association in 1976.

The available data on the psychological functioning of persons identified as homosexuals lead to an unambiguous conclusion: that the range of variation in personal adjustment is no different from that of heterosexuals (Ohlson, 1974). A review of 14 major studies, beginning with Hooker's in-depth investigation (1957, 1965), gave no support to the hypothesis that same-gender orientation was a sickness (Freedman, 1976). Employing various adjustment criteria, the studies uncovered no correlations that would support a mental illness construction. Siegleman (1978 & 1979), in two studies comparing psychological adjustment of homosexual men and women and heterosexual men and women in Britain, found no significant difference between the homosexual and heterosexual groups, substantially replicating the results of earlier studies in the U.S. The conclusion had been stated earlier in the famous Wolfenden Report of 1957, the basis for the repeal of sodomy statutes in England:

> homosexuality cannot legitimately be regarded as a disease because in many cases it is the only symptom and is compatible with full mental health (p. 32).

The Minority Group Construction--Homosexuals as a Non-Ethnic Minority Group.

The civil libertarian movements of the 1960s and 1970s paved the way for an alternative construction of homosexual conduct. We have already noted that the earlier work of Kinsey and his associates (1948) had received wide publicity. This work helped to strengthen the notion that sexual status and behavior could not be sorted into a simple two-valued model of normal and abnormal. The recognition that perhaps at least 10 percent of the adult population consistently adopted nonconforming sexual roles (i.e., homosexual behavior) was instrumental in formulating a construction of same-gender sexuality as the defining property of a nonethnic, nonracial minority group. Individuals came together to support each other in their choice of life style. They

17

comprised a group. They shared with other minority groups the painful and often humiliating experiences of discrimination, harassment, and rejection (Sagarin, 1971).

The model for conceptualizing homosexuals as a minority group was provided first by ethnic and racial minorities, later by nonethnic minorities: women, the aged, and physically disabled or handicapped persons. Another development that encouraged the use of the minority construction arose from claims that homosexual men and women could satisfactorily perform an infinite variety of occupational and recreational roles: one could have nonconforming sexual attitudes and still meet high performance standards as teachers, physicians, fire fighters, novelists, professional athletes, movie actors, policemen, politicians, judges and so on.

It would be instructive to review the features that define a minority group. It is obvious that "minority" in this context carries no quantitative meaning. Women make up more than 50 percent of the population, yet they meet the criteria of a minority group. The most useful shorthand definition of minority group is: people who share the experience of being the objects of discrimination on the basis of stereotypes, ethnocentric beliefs, and prejudice held by members of the nonminority group. Well-known examples are mid-nineteenth century Irish immigrants in Boston, American Indians for nearly four centuries, black soldiers and sailors prior to the anti-segregation orders, Asian-Americans before the repeal of the exclusion acts, Mexican-Americans in California and the Southwest, Jews in Nazi Germany and elsewhere.

Similarities to more widely recognized minority groups are not hard to find. Prejudice against persons with nonconforming sexual orientations is like racial prejudice in that stereotypes are created. Such stereotypes are often exaggerations of social types that feature some unwanted conduct, style of speech, manner, or style that purportedly differs from the prototype of the majority. The personality of an individual identified as a member of a minority group is construed not from his acts, but from his suspected or actual membership in the minority group. Racial and ethnic slurs help to maintain the partition between the minority group and the majority. Wops, Guineas, Japs, Spics, Kikes, Beaners, Polacks, Sambos, and other pejoratives have only recently been discouraged as terms to denote the social and moral inferiority of selected minority groups. Fag, fairy, queer, homo, and pervert serve similar functions for persons who want to communicate that the homosexual is "inferior." At the same time, the slur is intended to characterize a social type that exemplifies a negatively valued prototype--the feminized male.

18

Regulatory Policies in the Military

In the previous pages, we have provided an overview of changing folkways, of scientific findings, and of variations in the social construction of nonconforming sexuality. Our intention was to lay the groundwork for examining current policies that pertain to the suitability for military service of men and women who are not exclusively heterosexual.

In our examination of current policies, we are constrained to use language that is not consonant with our conclusion that sexuality is a multidimensional concept. If we were writing a scientific treatise on sexuality per se, we would make precise distinctions and note differences between biological role, gender identity, sexual practices, and sexual-social role. From such a perspective, the use of two broad classes, heterosexual and homosexual, would be extremely arbitrary. Because our objective is to illuminate the dark corners of sexuality for a particular policy purpose, we must make use of the language currently employed. Unless qualified in the text, when we employ the words "homosexual" and "heterosexual," we are complying with the more common current legalistic, categorical usage.

The Office of the Secretary of Defense formulated a concise summary of official policy (Department of Defense, 1982) as follows:

> Homosexuality is incompatible with military service. The presence of such members adversely affects the ability of the Armed Forces to maintain discipline, good order, and morale; to foster mutual trust and confidence among the members; to ensure the integrity of the system of rank and command; to facilitate assignment and worldwide deployment of members who frequently must live and work under close conditions affording minimal privacy; to recruit and retain members of the military services; to maintain the public acceptability of military services; and, in certain circumstances, to prevent breaches of security.

Appendix A reproduces DoD Directive 5200.2.R, which contains the current policy regarding granting clearances to homosexual men and women.

Since homosexuality is an abstract term (not unlike "heterosexuality"), the policy can only be implemented if positive criteria are formulated. Such criteria are to be found in the Uniform Code of Military Justice (UCMJ), set forth in the Manual for Courts

---

Martial (MCM),* a book of rules for dealing with criminal acts. In addition, various directives of the Department of Defense guide the procedures for the administrative separation of servicemen and women who are charged with homosexuality.

In the UCMJ, offenses are spelled out in various articles. Not only are the offenses named, but the legal criteria are established. For example, sodomy, a term that has been employed to denote many forms of nonprocreative sex, is defined in Article 125 as follows:

> It is unnatural carnal copulation for a person to take into the person's mouth or anus the sexual organ of another person or of an animal; or to place that person's organ in the mouth or anus of another person or an animal; or to have carnal copulation in any opening of the body, except the sexual parts, with another person; or to have carnal copulation with an animal (MCM, p. IV-90).

> Any person...who engages in unnatural carnal copulation with another person of same or opposite sex or with an animal is guilty of sodomy. Penetration, however slight, is sufficient to complete the offense (MCM, p. IV-90).

Another article (Article 134) addresses "indecency" defined as:

> that form of immorality relating to sexual impurity which is not only grossly vulgar, obscene, and repugnant to common propriety, but tends to excite lust and deprave the morals with respect to sexual relations (MCM, p. IV-131).

Although the intention of the articles is to provide clear definitions for criminal acts, some of the terms are ambiguous, for example, "unnatural," "sexual impurity," and "deprave the morals." These terms are drawn from remote sources that supplied the authors and translators of the Bible with guides to rule-making. Contemporary legal and linguistic analysis of these articles would lead to the deletion of rhetorical terms that could not be supported by empirical observation. The indecency article might be applied, for example, to the viewing of X-rated movies and other milder sexually stimulating materials on the grounds that they "excite lust."

---

*Manual for Courts Martial, Executive Order 12473, 13 Jul 1984.

20

Both the sodomy and the indecency articles are applicable to heterosexual as well as to homosexual acts. The sodomy article, as written, proscribes heterosexual nonvaginal intercourse. For example, oral-genital contact would be a criminal offense subject to severe punishment. The article does not distinguish between married and unmarried partners. As currently used in military law, the sodomy charge is employed far more often in cases of heterosexual behavior, and the total number of such charges is small. For example, in the U.S. Army during fiscal years 1987 through April of FY 1988, there were 178 sodomy charges, 174 offenders were male and 127 victims were female, 54 of those cases being consensual (W. S. Fulton, U.S. Army Clerk of Court, personal communication, May 1988).

A review of contemporary authorities on sexology, marriage, and family relations would raise questions about the UCMJ's criminalization of oral-genital sex play, especially since this is practiced by a large percentage of the general population (Katchadourian & Lunde, 1975). Since military personnel are drawn from the general population, it is reasonable to assume that large numbers of military men and women, married and unmarried, are in violation of the sodomy statute. If enforced, Article 125 would lead to punitive actions, including courts-martial, for an untold number of military personnel.

Recent DoD statistics on separations from the armed services for "homosexuality" provide an empirical basis for reconsidering traditional policies (Appendix B). We have assembled data for the fiscal years 1985, 1986, and 1987 for the various services. The data are not strictly comparable to the data extensively reported by Williams and Weinberg (1971) because of different record-keeping methods. Nevertheless, looking back over the past 20 years or more, it is incontrovertible that there has been a dramatic decrease in the rate of punitive discharges for homosexuality.

For the Army, during the three-year period, 829 enlisted men and 11 officers were separated administratively for homosexuality. During the same period, 354 enlisted women and 3 officers were separated. More revealing and more useful for policy decisions are the percentages: for men, .046 percent (less than 5 in 10,000); for women .17 percent (17 in 10,000).

For the Navy, the numbers are higher. For the three-year period, 1825 enlisted men and 30 officers were separated. All were handled administratively except for one enlisted man and one officer who were subject to courts-martial. For women, 382 enlisted and 4 officers were separated. When reduced to percentages, .127 percent of males were administratively separated (almost 13 in 10,000), and .27 percent of women (27 in 10,000).

The Marine Corps, being a smaller service, reported 213 separations of enlisted men and 6 separations of officers. For women, 90 enlisted were separated. The

21

percentage for men was .04 (4 per 10,000), about the same as the Army figures. For women, the percentage was .33 (33 in 10,000), double the rate for the Army, and somewhat higher than for the Navy.

The figures for the Air Force show 644 separations of enlisted men, and 41 separations of male officers for the three-year period. For women, 220 enlisted and 7 officers were separated. The rate for men is similar to the Army and Marines, .043 percent (4.3 per 10,000), the rate for women is lower than for the other services, .01 percent (1 per 10,000).

If we look at separated homosexuals in terms of their security clearance, it becomes apparent that such homosexual service members are very likely to hold a security clearance. During the period 1981-1987, 4,914 men were separated from the Army and the Air Force on the grounds of homosexuality*. Of these, 40 percent of the Army sample and 50 percent of the Air Force sample held Secret or Top Secret security clearances. It is reasonable to suppose that background investigations had yielded no information that would indicate that the subjects were security risks. It is interesting to note that only 28 percent of the homosexual servicemen were discharged in their first year; 72 percent continued to serve at least two years before their employment was terminated. Almost 32 percent served more than three years, and 17 percent served at least five years before they were discharged because of homosexuality. If there were a connection between being a homosexual and potential for security violations, then current methods are grossly inefficient for identifying homosexuals in a timely fashion.

Returning to the separation rates for the services during the three-year period, the Navy has the highest rates for men, the Marine Corps for women. These differential rates pose some interesting problems. Are the rates related to differential enforcement in the various services? Are the work and living conditions in one service more conducive to identifying homosexuals? Do the services vary in the use of recruitment criteria? Is one branch of the service more attractive to homosexuals?

These between-service differences, however, are not as important as the overall findings--the small proportions of separations (from 1:10,000 to 33:10,000). If we take the estimates of same-gender preference for the general population supplied by Kinsey in 1948 or Mihalek in 1988, we would expect to find separation rates in the range 300:10,000 to 1,000:10,000. That is to say, unless nearly all men and women with nonconforming sexual identities and behaviors had been screened out before or during training, the enforcement of the ban on homosexuals was simply not effective. It is difficult not to conclude that a large number of undetected homosexual men and

---

*John Goral, Defense Manpower Data Center, April 1988, unpublished data.

22

women are performing their military roles satisfactorily and that their sexual conduct does not come to the attention of their commanders.*

To account for the large discrepancy between the actual number of separations and the expected number of men and women who have same-gender orientation, several hypotheses may be entertained.

(1) Men and women who identify themselves as homosexual do not enter military service. This hypothesis is difficult to sustain. Harry (1984) found that homosexual and heterosexual men were equally likely to have served in the military. Homosexual women were more likely than heterosexual women to have had military service. Weinberg and Williams in a sworn affidavit state: "the vast majority of homosexuals in the Armed Forces remain undiscovered by military authorities, and complete their service with honor" (see Gibson, 1978). Ruse (1988) wrote:

> Many soldiers, sailors and airmen are homosexual--and actively so. They do not get caught or prosecuted because they are discreet or lucky, or because authorities turn a blind eye. But the rules do exist, and every now and then some unfortunate gets enmeshed in the net (p. 240).

These statements imply that a large number of homosexuals serve in the Armed Forces.

(2) Men and women with same-gender interests inhibit the expression of sexuality during their tenure in the Armed Forces. This hypothesis is without foundation when we consider the age group involved and the increasing lack of celibacy among young adults.

(3) Men and women who enter military service continue to express their sexual interests. This applies to those who are exclusively heterosexual, those who are exclusively homosexual, and those who make up Kinsey's intermediate groups. They do not come to the attention of

---

*There is the continually nagging question of the definition of "a homosexual." Do a few homosexual acts , or even one, make an otherwise heterosexual person a homosexual? Conversely, most would agree that a few heterosexual acts by an otherwise exclusively homosexual person do not make this person a heterosexual. It seems inescapable that the persons labelled "homosexual" by the military services represent all degrees of homosexual orientation and have in common only the fact of being identified by the military as engaging in some form of homosexual behavior.

23

---

authorities because they are discreet, and they enact their sexual roles in private and off military bases. Any member of the Armed Forces, heterosexual or homosexual, might engage in conduct that would violate Article 125, the sodomy statute. But if he or she were discreet, the violation is unlikely to be discovered and no administrative or judicial action would be taken.

(4) Commanders by and large exercise discretion, whenever possible dealing with infractions in an informal way and avoiding the requirement of taking official action. With the recent softening of public attitudes, this hypothesis seems plausible.

The fact that only an infinitesimal percentage of men and women are identified as homosexuals leads to an inescapable inference. Many undetected homosexuals serve in the military, enlisted and officers, men and women. This conclusion holds even if we employ the most rigorous criterion, i.e., exclusively homosexual. It would be helpful to policy-makers to know if those who were administratively separated were discovered as a result of public or indiscreet acts, inadvertently, through gossip, or through intentional self-disclosure. It would also be helpful to know if the separation was related to violating the sodomy statute or the decency statute. The latter statute is usually invoked when a person publicly engages in acts that are aesthetically or morally offensive.

On the reasonable assumption that the number of military personnel who are homosexual may be as high as 10 percent, only a minute percentage are separated from the service. This discrepancy calls into question the usefulness of Article 125. It may be that the article is simply unenforceable. When a rule, regulation, or ordinance is unenforceable, it falls into disuse. Ordinarily, the legal principle of desuetude is applied to such laws, eventually deleting them from legal codes. (In Appendix B we have included tables showing the number of separations for homosexuality, by service, from 1959 to the present. The ratio of those separated to total military population appears to be fairly stable.)

The Traditional View in Light of the Previous Discussion

The argument against including homosexuals in military units is usually stated in terms of organizational effectiveness and discipline. Military men and women, like many civilians, must be able to work cooperatively to achieve organizational objectives. The generally accepted wisdom is that in battle or crisis situations, simple cooperation is not enough. The soldier's morale and fighting efficiency depends upon his knowing that other members of his unit are dependable and will enact their roles according to plan.

24

As a result of the co-dependency fostered by training requirements, space sharing, commensalism, common goals, and mutual trust and respect, the relationships among members of combat teams are like those of primary groups. Informal covenants, rather than orders, bond the members of the group. It has been commonly assumed that the existence of deep-seated prejudice against homosexuals as a class would be a barrier to the creation and development of attitudes that would foster cohesive relations.

Although not well-publicized, the available data all point to the conclusion that preservice background characterization and subsequent job performance of homosexuals in the military is satisfactory (Williams & Weinberg, 1971; McDaniel, 1989; Zuliani, 1986; Crittenden Report, 1957). Whether the presence of men or women identified as nonconforming in sexual orientation actually influences such features of military life as discipline, group morale, integrity, etc., can be set out as a hypothesis and tested directly and indirectly. Direct testing would involve integrating men who identify themselves as holding nonconforming sexual attitudes with men who are unselected for discriminatory attitudes. The same design can be used for women. Such testing would be similar to the testing carried out by research teams when black soldiers were integrated into formerly all-white platoons, battalions, or regiments. The intensity of prejudice against homosexuals may be of the same order as the prejudice against blacks in 1948, when the military was ordered to integrate.

The order to integrate blacks was first met with stout resistance by traditionalists in the military establishment. Dire consequences were predicted for maintaining discipline, building group morale, and achieving military organizational goals. None of these predictions of doom has come true. Social science specialists helped develop programs for combating racial discrimination, so that now the military services are leaders in providing equal opportunity for black men and women. It would be wise to consider applying the experience of the past 40 years to the integration of homosexuals.

Indirect evidence to establish whether homosexuals could be satisfactorily integrated can be derived from retrospective accounts of honorably discharged men and women who were homosexuals at the time of their service. In a 1967 study conducted by the Institute of Sex Research at the University of Indiana, of 458 male homosexuals, 214 had served in the military, of whom 77 percent received Honorable Discharges. A later study reported that of 136 homosexuals who had been in the military services, 76 percent received honorable discharges (Williams and Weinberg, 1971). Another study (Harry, 1984) analyzed interview data on 1,456 respondents, men and women, who had served in the military. Homosexual and heterosexual men were equally likely to have served in the military, while homosexual women were more likely than heterosexual women to have served. Nearly 80 percent of the homosexual personnel in these samples received honorable discharges.

25

It is not unreasonable to expect similar findings among more recent veterans. While there would be difficulties in locating these veterans, the effort could pay off in providing information about individual and group adjustment.

The argument has been put forth by Moskos (Morrison, 1988) that the number of homosexual men and women who are separated from the current All Volunteer Force comprise most of the homosexuals who enter the military services. The argument is based on the assumption that most homosexuals would avoid entering hostile occupational environments such as the military. Because most homosexual men and women acquire skill at masking, deception, and other self-presentation techniques to conceal their nonconformity, they would not need to avoid the employment opportunities offered by the military because of fear of detection. It is unlikely that the caricature of the male homosexual, the feminized male, would volunteer for military service, or be accepted. It is, however, estimated that such feminized males make up only a small proportion of homosexuals, perhaps 10 percent.

Thus, 90 percent of male homosexuals display no overt behavioral stigmata. In the interest of survival, practiced impression management makes it possible to conceal one's sexual preference whether in military or civilian settings. Also, Harry (1984) has suggested that some homosexuals do not declare their status at the time of recruitment because they do not know they are homosexual. "The median age of 'coming out' or fully realizing one's homosexuality and becoming socially and sexually active is approximately 19 or 20....This age coincides with the age when men traditionally entered the service..." (p. 121). Thus, some persons do not know of or act out their homosexual urges until after induction. Such people are most unlikely to be screened out at the time of entry into military service.

An additional mode of gaining indirect evidence would be the study of the experience of quasi-military organizations where integration has been achieved. Prior to the 1970s, the San Francisco Sheriff's Department, like most law-enforcement agencies, had embraced the customary discriminatory policies against homosexuals. At the time the personnel numbered 500. In 1979, an active campaign was set in motion to recruit homosexuals, and 10 homosexual officers were selected. In 1980, McIntyre conducted an in-depth study of the Department and reported that the homosexual members had 'above average' job performance ratings and had higher retention rates than nonhomosexuals. After the first year, the issue of gay colleagues was of little concern either to the deputies themselves or to the administrative officers. Both homosexual and heterosexual personnel took the position that sexual preference had nothing to do with the performance of professional duties. The success of the integration, according to McIntyre's analysis, was in large measure due to top management's strong support of anti-discrimination policies.

26

The current status in the Sheriff's Department is that sexual orientation is not an issue for hiring or continued employment. Statistics are no longer kept on the sexual orientation of personnel. It is estimated that 40 to 50 (about 10 percent) of the Sheriff's Department may be classified as homosexual. About a quarter of the force is made up of women, of whom about 10 percent are assumed to be homosexual (R. Dyer, personal communication, April 27, 1988).* The San Francisco Police Department initiated a similar nondiscrimination policy in 1979, as has the Los Angeles Police Department**. Most if not all law enforcement agencies in California are now hiring without regard to sexual orientation. Many believe that they are mandated by law to do so, as we pointed out on page 5.

Resistance to Change

In the foregoing analysis, we have tried to make the case that the military services should prepare for a shift in legal and public opinion on discrimination against homosexuals. Such a change in a time-honored practice is not likely to be accepted without active resistance. In the absence of compelling reasons, bureaucracies resist change. The first line of such resistance is the invocation of the concept of tradition. In general, the arguments against change contain declarations of the necessity for preserving such abstract qualities as integrity, morals, morale, pride, fidelity, and so on.

One of the more powerful reasons for rejecting change has to do with the idealized imagery of the combat soldier. Although unsupported by evidence, the belief is widely held that men must be rugged, tough, and macho to achieve success in battle. In the belief system of current traditional military authorities, homosexual men cannot be rugged, tough, and macho.*** The stereotype of homosexual men, as we mentioned earlier, centers on the feminized male who is unable to perform masculine tasks. It is interesting to note that this stereotype continues to flourish even though

---

*San Francisco Sheriff's Department

**Although the Los Angeles Police Department (LAPD) has an official policy of nondiscrimination against homosexuals and such discrimination is also forbidden in employment by the Los Angeles Municipal Code, a pervasive anti-homosexual bias is alleged to exist in the LAPD. Mitchell Grobeson, a homosexual former police sergeant claims in a five million dollar suit against the LAPD that he was discriminated against, abused, intimidated and had to resign because he feared for his life (Stewart, 1988).

***In Classical Greece homosexuality and homosexual bonds between soldiers were considered an asset to the performance of the fighting man in terms of patriotism and military courage.

27

female personnel now perform all manner of military tasks except combat, and it is well known that such "macho males" as motorcyclists of the Hell's Angels type and many tough prisoners in correctional settings engage in homosexual behavior.

A recent exchange in the Navy Times reflects a criticism of current policy and a vehement defense of traditional military attitudes. Under the heading, Man the barricades: The federal court is letting 'them' in, Michelle McCormick wrote a column poking fun at the arguments offered by supporters of discriminatory policies. Representative of her facetious bits of advice to future judges is the following:

> Homosexuals are likely to bother people who don't want to be bothered. The bothering that goes on now is between men and women. It is the right and natural way of things that men should bother women who would rather be left alone. But men are not accustomed to being bothered; and they shouldn't have to put up with it (Navy Times, 29 February 1988, p. 62).

Ms. McCormick's column brought forth a letter to the editor from Major Randel Webb, USMC, who strongly defended the traditional point of view. Major Webb wrote [in part]:

> Clearly she accepts a main plank of the homosexual community agenda that denies their own profoundly aberrant behavior. It promotes the idea they are just like everyone else except for sexual preference. There are valid reasons homosexuals should not be accepted into the military.
>
> Homosexuals are a politically active special interest group. The services have adopted policies opposing homosexuals primarily because they are a threat to good order and discipline.
>
> Most people, though Ms. McCormick would probably consider them unenlightened, loath homosexuals. Their contempt is easily recognizable in the form of derision and jokes. Homosexuals would be harassed, and discriminated against. What the armed services do not need, is another political body within itself to create dissension.
>
> There are also real problems like homosexuals demanding recognition of their marriages and thus base housing and BAQ* at the married rate, fraternization and all of its implications, morale and retention problems that would be caused by people who leave in disgust, and reduced effectiveness of homosexual officers and NCO's handling contemptuous subordinates. ...The pointed end of the armed forces have a critical mission to prepare for and conduct war. It requires teamwork, camaraderie, and a sense of pride in being associated with other members of the unit.
>
> These elements are achieved by several factors, among them are discipline and good order. Tolerating homosexuals in the armed forces is contrary to good order and discipline.

---

*Basic allowance for quarters

28

Most of the issues raised by Major Webb, which reflect traditional anti-homosexual arguments, are reminiscent of the issues raised when black athletes (then called Negro athletes) were first allowed to participate in professional baseball. Webb's concerns are also reminiscent of the arguments advanced against the 1948 order to desegregate military establishments, and the later arguments that sought to minimize the role of women in the Armed Forces. Despite its early resistance to change, it is important to repeat that the military establishment is now looked upon as a model for racial and gender integration.

In his list of problems that would be created if homosexuals were freely admitted into the services, Major Webb failed to mention potential security risks. This has been one of the main reasons given for screening out homosexual men and women from the military, and from jobs requiring a security clearance. The argument goes that they would be candidates for blackmail if a foreign agent learned that they were homosexuals. This argument is somewhat blunted when we remind ourselves that blackmail is also an option for foreign agents who acquire knowledge about heterosexual men or women secretly engaged in adultery. Also, decriminalizing homosexual behavior has done much to decrease the danger of blackmail.

Historical support for the notion that security concerns about homosexuals are exaggerated is contained in the 1957 Crittenden Report, officially labelled Report of the Board Appointed to Prepare and Submit Recommendations to the Secretary of the Navy for the Revision of Policies, Procedures and Directives Dealing with Homosexuals (Gibson, 1978). The Report contains the following remarks:

> The concept that homosexuals pose a security risk is unsupported by any factual data. Homosexuals are no more a security risk, and many cases are much less of a security risk, than alcoholics and those people with marked feelings of inferiority who must brag of their knowledge of secret information and disclose it to gain stature. Promiscuous heterosexual activity also provides serious security implications. Some intelligence officers consider a senior officer having illicit heterosexual relations with the wife of a junior officer or enlisted man is much more of a security risk than the ordinary homosexual....The number of cases of blackmail as a result of past investigations of homosexuals is negligible. No factual data exist to support the contention that homosexuals are a greater risk than heterosexuals.

In the 30 years since the Crittenden report was submitted, no new data have been presented that would refute its conclusion that homosexuals are not greater security risks than heterosexuals.

29

To return to the discussion of official policy as presented by Major Webb, the style of his arguments does not reflect the small but historically significant changes in practice. Webb's rhetoric supporting discrimination implies punitive measures for homosexual personnel. However, in the three-year period, 1985-87, only two of the military persons charged with sodomy were specifically identified as homosexual and separated as such by courts-martial. Since the policy changes introduced in 1981, almost 100 percent of homosexual separations have been administrative, and 55 percent of these separations have been characterized as honorable. This indicates a softening of attitudes.

The psychological and sociological literature contains abundant documentation for the correlation between tolerance of, and knowledge about, minorities. Such knowledge is most often acquired through social exposure and education (Allport, 1954; Pettigrew, 1969). The implication of this correlation is that prejudice is nurtured by ignorance. A corollary of this implication is the formula: ignorance - prejudice - avoidance - ignorance. If individuals physically or psychologically partition themselves from a certain class of people, they cannot help but remain ignorant of evidence that might disconfirm their prejudices.

The unreasoned resistance to learning about or interacting with homosexuals has led to the formulation of the concept of homophobia. Some men experience uneasy feelings when in close proximity to other men who are identified as homosexuals. It is as if such nearness could pollute one's identity. The term, homophobia, is used in parallel with terms for other phobias connoting unreasoned fear and avoidance of certain classes of objects, such as zoophobia (fear of animals), agoraphobia (fear of open spaces), mysophobia (fear of dirt), etc.

Some degree of homophobia has been a part of the conventional attitude structure of American males. It is based on entrenched religious beliefs, folklore, and stereotypes. Such attitudes are connected to the heroic and positively valued image of the powerful, virile heterosexual male and the degraded and negatively valued image of the powerless, weak, feminized, homosexual male.

One of the strong motivations reinforcing homophobia is the need to disown the possibility of having homosexual interests. Even a momentary questioning of one's sexual status might lead to the anxious consideration that "I might become one." Such a silent thought might lead the uncertain male to take action to convince himself and others that his identity is not homosexual. Such action may be violent, as in "gay bashing," or relatively benign, as in purposeful avoidance. The psychological process involved is called reaction formation. By taking a public stand against the expression of homosexual conduct by others, the man secretly unsure of his own identity conquers his doubts. Overt acts of discrimination become the means of publicly convincing

30

others and privately convincing himself of his highly valued masculinity (Weinberg, 1973).

Those who resist changing the traditional policies support their position with statements of the negative effects on discipline, morale, and other abstract values of military life. Buried deep in the supporting conceptual structure is the fearful imagery of homosexuals polluting the social environment with unrestrained and wanton expressions of deviant sexuality. It is as if persons with nonconforming sexual orientations were always indiscriminately and aggressively seeking sexual outlets. All the studies conducted on the psychological adjustment of homosexuals that we have seen lead to contrary inferences. The amount of time devoted to erotic fantasy or to overt sexual activity varies greatly from person to person and is unrelated to gender preference (Kinsey, Pomeroy, and Martin, 1948; Hooker, 1965; Freedman, 1976; Williams and Weinberg, 1971). In one carefully conducted study, homosexuals actually demonstrated a lower level of sexual interest than heterosexuals (Bell, 1973).

Homosexuals are like heterosexuals in being selective in their choice of partners, in observing rules of privacy, in considering appropriateness of time and place, in connecting sexuality with the tender sentiments, and so on. To be sure, some homosexuals are like some heterosexuals in not observing privacy and propriety rules. In fact, the manifold criteria that govern sexual interest are identical for homosexuals and heterosexuals, save for only one criterion: the gender of the sexual partner.

Age, gender, kinship, class membership, marital status, size and shape, social role, posture, manners, speech, clothing, interest/indifference signalling, and other physical and behavioral criteria are all differentiating cues. They serve as filters to screen out undesirable or unsuitable potential sex partners. With such an array of cues, many (in some cases, all) potential objects of interest are rejected. For most people, only a small number of potential partners meet the manifold criteria. Whether in an Army platoon or in a brokerage office, people are generally selective in their choice of intimate partners and in their expression of sexual behavior. Heterosexuals and homosexuals alike employ all these variables in selecting partners, the only difference being that the latter include same-gender as a defining criterion, the former include opposite-gender.

In recent years, traditionalists have pointed to the AIDS crisis as a cogent reason for maintaining the discriminatory policies. Clearly all responsible persons are concerned about AIDS as a critical health problem, whether in government, in the military, or in the private sector. AIDS is a serious public health problem. When the disease was first identified in 1981, it was often called the "homosexual disease" and the "gay plague." Because no preparatory information had been given the public, the belief quickly spread that AIDS was exclusively a disease of homosexuals (Quaddland and Shattes, 1987). Subsequent research and observation has confirmed that everyone is

31

susceptible to the disease. The highest risk groups are needle-sharing intravenous substance users and homosexual men. Currently, of 70,702* cases in the United States, 43,679 (61.78%) are homosexual or bisexual men, 13,273 (18.77%) are intravenous drug users, 5,093 (7.20%) are intravenous drug users and also homosexual or bisexual males. Some 2,920 (4.13%) are heterosexual.

To date, the statistics tell us that AIDS is indeed at this time principally a disease of homosexual men and intravenous drug users, but changes in the epidemiological pattern are likely. In Haiti and Central Africa, AIDS is now transmitted mainly through heterosexual contact (Sulima, 1987). Currently, it is estimated by the Centers for Disease Control (CDC) that 1.0-1.5 million persons in the United States have been exposed to the Human Immunodeficiency Virus (HIV) and are "HIV positive." Most of these cases are undiagnosed and show few if any symptoms. The proportion of homosexuals to heterosexuals in the total HIV positive group is unknown.

From the data at hand, male homosexuals remain at much higher risk than do heterosexuals. Current medical diagnostic and treatment practices are rational, given contemporary medical knowledge. All military personnel are subject to HIV testing. If a person is tested positive, he or she is fully evaluated and then monitored by medical staff. Such a person continues to perform his or her duties until such time as disabling symptoms appear. Medical discharge is then the rule. Whether he or she is homosexual is not at issue. Controversy may be expected, however, in connection with recruiting. All recruits are now tested for HIV, and those who test positive are rejected. An unknown proportion of those tested positive will not develop the disease (and some of the HIV positive tests may be in error, i.e., false positives). Since AIDS is not contagious in the course of normal occupational and recreational activity, an argument could be made that HIV-positivity is not a fair criterion for rejection. The military must weigh the costs of rejecting large numbers of HIV positives (an unknown percentage of whom would not develop the disease) against the medical costs of monitoring and treatment of those who turn out to develop symptoms.

---

*As of August 15, 1988, 39,898 (56.43%) had died. (These data were acquired via personal communication with a staff member of the Centers for Disease Control [CDC] in Atlanta.)

32

Summary and Implications

An examination of recent social and political history points to the fact that the courts are slowly moving toward eliminating discrimination on the basis of nonconforming sexual orientation. Active citizen groups and lobbies provide support for advocates of nondiscrimination. Our studied conclusion is that the military services will soon be asked by the courts or the Congress to reexamine their policies and practices regarding recruitment and retention of men and women whose sexual interests deviate from the customary. This will become a burning issue if it is necessary to resort to drafting young persons for military service because of a decreasing supply of volunteers. Under prevailing social conditions, a public admission of homosexuality carries less stigma than in earlier times, and is no legal bar to most employment. Thus, unless the military is willing to adopt nondiscriminatory policies, a mere claim of homosexuality, whether true or false, would excuse any person who wants to avoid military service.

Our analysis directs us to regard people with nonconforming sexual orientation as a minority group. Our nation has a long history of successfully dealing with minority groups, particularly ethnic minorities. In the recent past, we have also learned how to integrate racial and other minority groups, notably women, into nearly every aspect of political and social life. The suggestion that we perceive homosexual men and women as a minority group follows from our analysis of contemporary scientific social and legal observations. The social construction of homosexuals as minority group members is more in tune with current behavioral science theory than the earlier constructions: sin, crime, and sickness. Our digest of the available body of scientific knowledge led to another implication: that the uncritical use of binary categories does violence to the findings reported by scientific observers. The rigid categories, heterosexual and homosexual, although necessary for certain purposes, are inadequate to reflect the complexity of the multidimensional antecedents of sexual status. Constructing a catalog of the variety of biological and socio-sexual types is less important than finding answers to questions of this form: Does atypical sexual orientation influence job performance? Studies of homosexual veterans make clear that having a same-gender or an opposite-gender orientation is unrelated to job performance in the same way as is being left- or right-handed (Williams & Weinberg, 1971).

For the purpose of military organization, however, quality of job performance may be less important than the effects of homosexuals (minority group members) on that important but ephemeral quality: group cohesion. The important question to be raised in future research must center on the claims that persons with nonconforming sexual attitudes create insurmountable problems in the maintenance of discipline, group cohesion, morale, organizational pride, and integrity.

In our study of suitability for military service, we have been governed by a silent assumption: that social attitudes are historically conditioned. In our own time, we have

33

---

witnessed far-reaching changes in attitudes toward the physically disabled, people of color, disease prevention, birth control, cohabitation of unmarried couples, and so on. We have witnessed a noticeable shift in tolerance for women and for homosexual men and women in the civilian workplace.

As a way of conceptualizing shifting social attitudes, we have developed a heuristic model.' Like all models, it is intended to simplify complex propositions, graphically portraying multiple concepts so they may be perceived simultaneously. The categories on the vertical are "customary" and "different," on the horizontal, lawful and unlawful.

34

In the spirit of a heuristic model, the categories are suggestive, not precise. The large rectangle embraces conduct in general, the interior rectangle represents sexual conduct. The horizontal line and the vertical line are boundaries between classes of conduct. The lines are broken to indicate permeability. That is to say, classification of social acts, under certain conditions, can be moved through the boundary from one cell to another.

The horizontal line separates customary ("normal") social acts from acts that are not customary, ("different"). The term "different" is superordinate to the often-used "deviant." Our current speech conventions give "different" its meaning from the notion of relative frequency. "Deviant" adds a pejorative value judgment to the meaning. "Customary" and "different" should be perceived as regions on a dimension. Some acts are more "different" than others. In the interest of simplicity, however, we write of "customary" and "different" as discrete classes. Political, economic, and moral conditions influence the sorting of social acts as customary or different.

The vertical boundary is also permeable; it separates lawful and unlawful acts. At time$_1$ certain acts are lawful but different (Cell III). Ordinary language terms to denote such acts are "attention-getting," "eccentric," and "far-out." An example would be flagpole-sitting. Because of hazards in connection with traffic control of curious drivers, a municipality enacts an ordinance making flagpole-sitting a misdemeanor. At time$_2$, then, flagpole-sitting has been reclassified to Cell IV, different and unlawful. Judicial decisions and legislative acts provide the criteria for reclassifying any particular social act along the horizontal axis (lawful-unlawful).

Cell I contains most of our everyday acts. We conduct ourselves according to custom and according to law. Cell II is populated by social acts that are widely practiced but unlawful, such as exceeding speed limits, jaywalking, tax evasion, driving "under the influence," etc. Cell III is populated by social acts which are currently lawful, but not widely practiced, such as flagpole-sitting, alligator-wrestling, and wearing "outlandish" costumes. In the 1930s women took to wearing trousers when trousers were considered properly part of men's attire. At that time, such "eccentric" acts were classified in Cell III, different but not unlawful. In earlier times, cross-dressing had been assigned to Cell IV. In New England, as late as the nineteenth century cross-dressing was a crime. The contents of the criminal code had been formed from Scriptural injunctions, among them:

> A woman shall not wear anything that pertains to a man nor shall a man put on a woman's garment; for whoever does these things is an abomination to Yahweh your God (Deuteronomy 22:5).

35

The social acts that are included in Cell IV would be specified in criminal codes and in less formal codes that identify "deviance." The fact that large numbers of criminal offenses are perpetrated every day does not qualify such acts for inclusion in Cells I or II. They are not customary, even though rates of crime are on the rise.

When a criminal statute is repealed, social acts that had been classified as different and unlawful (Cell IV) are reclassified in Cell III. This was the case when the Prohibition Amendment was repealed in 1932. Subsequently, the social act of manufacturing and selling alcoholic beverages rapidly moved into Cell I, customary and lawful.

The interior rectangle is central to our interest in conceptualizing the varieties of sexual behavior. The horizontal and vertical broken lines denote permeable boundaries to create four classes. Cell A is the customary and lawful form of heterosexual congress between two consenting adults in the "missionary" position--face to face. Cell B contains those acts which are illegal but are frequently practiced. This would include (in some States) oral-genital sex play between consenting heterosexuals, adultery, and fornication with a consenting minor.* Cell C would include such acts as socially condoned voyeurism (viewing topless dancers), fetishism, Don Juanism, collecting pornographic photographs. Cell D contains those deviant sexual behaviors that are contained in various criminal codes, such as pedophilia, bestiality, public indecency, lust murders, rape (hetero- or homosexual), and in some States, consensual sodomy (hetero- or homosexual).

For social acts in general, we have illustrated how certain acts can be reassigned as the result of changing attitudes and or legislation. The same formulation applies to the subdivision of social acts that we call sexual acts. For example, it is commonplace, i.e., "customary," now for persons to rent or buy sexually explicit videotapes. Not too long ago, such acts would have been declared "different" and unlawful. More recently, such acts were considered lawful and different (Cell C). Changing folkways regarding nudity and sexuality are influencing the public to assign such acts to Cell I. Of the acts included in Cell D, consensual sexual acts between same-gender persons continue to be unlawful in half the United States. At one time, such acts were unlawful in all the States. Changes in public attitudes and legislation have resulted in such homosexual acts between consenting adults being shifted from Cell D to Cell C. As we detailed before, in many segments of society (e.g., California law-enforcement and other public agencies, and most major corporations) sexual orientation has become a matter of indifference. For these segments of society, homosexual acts have been reclassified from Cell D to Cell C (different but lawful).

---

*as distinct from child molestation.

36

It should be emphasized that although the vertical boundary is permeable, it is not permeable to all acts. Sexual acts that involve children, violence, or public indecency, i.e., criminal offenses, are not likely to be reclassified. Such offenses tear the very fabric of social order.

Our purpose in presenting this model is to make clear that the values that any society places on social acts are subject to change. The model is consistent with an underlying premise that we live in an ever-changing dynamic world. The lessons of history tell us that the legitimacy of our behaviors, customs, and laws is not permanently resistant to change. Custom and law change with the times, sometimes with amazing rapidity. The military cannot indefinitely isolate itself from the changes occurring in the wider society, of which it is an integral part.

References

Allport, G. W. (1954). The nature of prejudice. Cambridge, MA: Addison-Wesley.

American Forces Press Service (1988, April 18). DoD's homosexual policy unchanged. American Forces Press Service, Press & Art Pack #16.

Barnett, W. (1973). Sexual freedom and the Constitution. Albuquerque, NM: U. of New Mexico Press.

Bell, A. P. (1973). Homosexualitites: Their range and character. Nebraska Symposium on Motivation, 21, 1-26.

Bell, A. P., & Weinberg, M. S. (1978). Homosexualities. New York: Simon & Schuster.

Bieber, I., Dain, H. J., Dince, P. R., Drellich, M. G., Grand, H. G., Gundlach, R. H., Kremer, M. W., Rifkin, A. H., Wilbur, C. B., & Bieber, T. B. (1962). Homosexuality, a psychoanalytic study. New York, NY: Basic Books.

Bishop, K. (1988, June 10). Court to rehear challenge to Army's homosexual ban. New York Times, p. A8.

Brzek, A., & Hubalek, S. (1988). Homosexuals in Eastern Europe: Mental health and psychotherapy issues. Journal of Homosexuality, 15, 1-2.

Bullough, V. L. (1976). Sexual variance in society and history. Chicago, IL: University of Chicago Press.

Devereaux, G. (1963). Institutionalized homosexuality of the Mohave Indians. In Ruitenbeck, H. (Ed.), The problem of homsexuality. New York: Dutton.

Department of Defense. (1982, January 28). DoD Directive 1332.14.

Egelko, B. (1988, Oct. 13). Judicial panel hear arguments against Army homosexual policy. The Herald of the Monterey Peninsula, p. 74.

Ellis, H. (1915). Studies in the psychology of sex, Vol. 2: Sexual inverson. Philadelphia: F. A. Davis.

Ellis, L., & Ames, M.A. (1987). Neurohormonal functioning and sexual orientation: A theory of homosexuality-heterosexuality. Psychological Bulletin, 101(2), 233-258.

Ford, C.S., & Beach, F.A. (1951). The patterns of sexual behavior. New York: Harper & Brothers.

39

Freedman, A. M., Kaplan, H. I., & Sadock, B. J. (1975). Comprehensive Textbook of Psychiatry/II. Baltimore: Williams & Wilkins.

Freedman, M. (1976). Homosexuality and psychological functioning. Belmont, CA: Brooks/Cole.

Freud, S. (1938). The basic writings of Sigmund Freud. Brill, A.A. (trans.). New York: Modern Library. (Original work published 1905)

Geis, G., Wright, R., Garrett, R., & Wilson, P.R. (1976). Reported consequences of decriminalization of consensual adult homosexuality in seven American States. Journal of Homosexuality, 1, 419-426.

Gibson, E. L. (1978). Get off my ship. New York: Avon. Appendix E contains the 1957 Crittenden Report.

Guevarra, L. (1988, February 11). U.S. Court overturns Army's ban on gays. San Francisco Chronicle.

Harry, J. (1984). Homosexual men and women who served their country. Journal of Homosexuality, 10(1-2), 117

Hefner, H. M. (1964, April 1). The Playboy philosophy (editorial). Playboy.

Henry, W. A. (1988, February 22). Uniform treatment for gays. Time, p. 55.

High Tech Gays, et. al. v. Defense Industrial Security Clearance Office, 56 U.S. L.W. 2144 (1987).

Homosexual Sergeant. (1975, June 9). Time, pp. 18-19.

Hooker, E. (1957). The adjustment of the male overt homosexual. Journal of Projective Techniques, 21, 18.

Hooker, E. (1965). Male homosexuals and their worlds. In Marmor, J. (Ed.), Sexual inversions, 83-103. New York: Basic Books.

Howells, K. (Ed.) (1984). The psychology of sexual diversity. Oxford: Basil Blackwell.

Kallman, F.J. (1952). A comparative twin study on the genetic aspects of male homosexuality. Journal of Nervous and Mental Diseases, 115, p. 283.

Katchadourian, H.A., & Lunde, D.T. (1975). Fundamentals of human sexuality, II edition. New York: Holt, Rinehart & Winston.

40

Kelly, D.D. (1985). Sexual differentiation of the nervous system. In Kandel, E., & Schwartz, J. (Eds.), Principles of neural science, 2nd edition. New York: Elsevier.

Kinsey, A., Pomeroy, W., & Martin, C. (1948). Sexual behavior in the human male. Philadelphia: W. B. Saunders & Co.

Kinsey, A., Pomeroy, W., Martin, C., & Gebhard, P. (1953). Sexual behavior in the human female. Philadelphia: W. B. Saunders & Co.

Klein, F., & Wolf, T. J. (1985). Introduction. Journal of Homosexuality, 11, 1-5.

Kolodny, R.C., Masters, W.H., & Johnson, W.E. (1979). Textbook of sexual medicine. Boston: Little, Brown & Co.

Krafft-Ebing, R. (von) (1922). Psychopathia Sexualis (F.J. Rebman, Trans.). Brooklyn, NY: Physicians & Surgeons Book Co. (Original work published 1880)

Law, S. A. (1988). Homosexuality and the social meaning of gender. Wisconsin Law Review, Volume 1988, No. 2, 187-235.

Livingood, J. M. (Ed.) (1976). National Institute of Mental Health Task Force on Homosexuality. Rockville, MD: National Institute of Mental Health.

MacDonald, A. P. (1982). Bisexuality: Some comments on research and theory. Journal of Homosexuality, 6, 21-30.

Marmor, J. (1975). Homosexuality and sexual orientation disturbances. In Freedman, A.M., Kaplan, H.I., & Sadock, B.J. (Eds.), Comprehensive textbook of psychiatry-II. Baltimore, MD: Williams & Wilkins.

Marshall, D.S., & Suggs, R.C. (Eds.). (1971). Human sexual behavior. New York: Basic Books.

Matlovich v. Secretary of the Air Force. 47 U.S. Law Week 2631, (D.C. Ct. App., Dec. 6, 1978).

Maze, R. (1988, June 13). VA extending benefits to more homosexual veterans. Navy Times, p. 14.

McCormick, M. (1988, February 29). Man the barricades, the federal court is letting "them" in. Navy Times, p. 62.

41

McDaniel, M. A. (1989). Preservice adjustment of homosexual and heterosexual military accessions: Implications for security clearance suitability (PERS-TR-89-004). Report in preparation. Monterey, CA: Defense Personnel Security Research and Education Center.

McIntyre, M. T. (1980). Homosexuality and the U.S. military. Master's thesis, Naval Postgraduate School, Monterey, CA.

Mihalek, G.J. (1988, January). Sexuality and gender, an evolutionary perspective. Psychiatric Annals. 18(1).

Money, J. (1988). Gay, straight & in-between. New York: Oxford University Press.

Money, J., & Erhardt, A.A. (1972). Man and woman, boy and girl. Baltimore, MD: Johns Hopkins University Press.

Morrison, D. (1988, March 5). Are homosexuals bad soldiers? National Journal, pp. 604-605.

National Security Institute. (1987, September). Court rules for gays. National Security Institute Advisory, 3(2), p. 84.

Norton v. Macy. 417 F.2d 1161 (D.C. Cir. 1969).

Ohlson, E.L. (1974). A preliminary investigation into the self-disclosing ability of male homosexuals. Psychology, 11, 21-25.

Paul, J. P. (1985). Bisexuality: Reassessing our paradigms of sexuality. Journal of Homosexuality, 11, 21-31.

Pettigrew, T.F. (1969). Racially separate or together? Journal of Social Issues. 25, 43-69.

Quaddland, M.C., & Shattes, W.D. (1987). AIDS sexuality and sexual control. Journal of Homosexuality, 14(1-2).

Rosa, P.M. (1988, July 12). Homosexuals no longer face automatic ban as security risks. The Morning Call.

Rosen, I. (Ed.) (1979). Sexual deviation. Oxford: Oxford University Press.

Ruse, M. (1988). Homosexuality, a philosophic inquiry. New York: Blackwell.

42

Sagarin, E. (Ed.) (1971). The other minorities. Waltham, MA: Ginn & Co.

Siegleman, M. (1978). Psychological adjustment of homosexual and heterosexual men: A cross national replication. Archives of Sexual Behavior, 7, 1-11.

Siegleman, M. (1979). Adjustment of homosexual and heterosexual women: A cross-national replication. Archives of Sexual Behavior, 8(2), 121-125.

Singer v. U.S. Civil Service Commission, 530 F.2d 247 (9th Cir. 1975).

Singer v. U.S. Civil Service Commission, 429 U.S. 1034 (1977).

Spector, M. & Kitsuse, J. I. (1987). Constructing social problems. New York: Aldine-de Gruyter.

Stein, T.J. (1976). Gay service organizations: A survey. Homosexual Counseling Journal, 3, 84-97.

Stewart, R. W. (1988, Sept. 29). Forced to quit, gay ex-officer charges in suit. Los Angeles Times.

Stuart, T., Jr. (1988, June 16). Dismissal of gay CIA worker is subject to review, court holds. New York Times, pp. A1, D24.

Sulima, J.P. (1987). What every drug counsellor should know about AIDS. Washington, DC: Morrisses Communication Group.

The Wolfenden Report (1963, orig. 1957). Report of the Committee on Homosexual Affairs and Prostitution. New York: Stein and Ray.

U.S. Commission on Civil Rights (1977, August 15).

Vetri, D. (1980). The legal arena: Progress for gay civil rights. Journal of Homosexuality 5, 25-34.

Webb, R. (1988, April 4). Real problems [Letter to the editor]. Navy Times, p. 23.

Webster, William H., Director of Central Intelligence Petitioner v. John Doe, 48 S.Ct. (1988)

Weinberg, G. (1973). Society and the healthy homosexual. Garden City, NY: Anchor Books.

43

Williams, C.I., & Weinberg, M.S. (1971). Homosexuals and the military. New York: Harper and Row.

Zuliani, R.A. (1986). Annexes to Charter Task Force Final Report (Annexes A-F to part 4). Canadian Department of National Defense.

44

List of Appendixes

A. The Legal Status of Homosexuality

B. Military Service Separation for Homosexuality

C. Statistical Data on Homosexuality

D. Bisexuality

45

APPENDIX A

The Legal Status of
Homosexuality

A-0

The Legal Status of
Homosexuality

This appendix summarizes current DoD laws and regulations which address homosexuality and homosexual behavior. There is also a brief overview of current civilian criminal law concerning homosexuality.

The appendix is organized as follows:

A-1

I. Current DoD Policy

The DoD policy on homosexuality announced by the Office of the Secretary of Defense is implemented through the Uniform Code of Military Justice (UCMJ) which addresses criminal acts, and through DoD directives which cover the administrative separation of service members for homosexuality. There are also specific separate regulations for each of the military services which are derived from the DoD directives.

A. Uniform Code of Military Justice

The punitive articles in the UCMJ which address homosexual and other criminal sexual activity are:

Article 80   - attempts

Article 125   - sodomy

Article 134   - assault with intent to commit sodomy

Article 134   - indecent assault

Article 134   - indecent acts with another

A-2

<u>Text</u>

An act, done with specific intent to commit an offense under this chapter, amounting to more than mere preparation and tending, even though failing, to effect its commission, is an attempt to commit that offense.

<u>Elements</u>

(1)   That the accused did a certain overt act;

(2)   That the act was done with specific intent to commit a certain offense under the code;

(3)   That the act amounted to more than mere preparation; and

(4)   That the act apparently tended to effect the commission of the intended offense.

Explanation. To constitute an attempt there must be a specific intent to commit the offense accompanied by an overt act which directly tends to accomplish the unlawful purpose. Preparation consists of devising or arranging the means or measures necessary for the commission of the offense. The overt act required goes beyond preparatory steps and is a direct movement toward the commission of the offense.

<u>Maximum punishment</u>

A person found guilty of an attempt shall be subject to the same maximum punishment authorized for the commission of the offense attempted, except that in no case shall the death penalty or confinement exceeding 20 years be adjudged.

A-3

Article 125 - Sodomy

<u>Text</u>

Any person subject to this chapter who engages in unnatural carnal copulation with another person of the same or opposite sex or with an animal is guilty of sodomy. Penetration, however slight, is sufficient to complete the offense.

<u>Elements</u>

(1) That the accused engaged in unnatural carnal copulation with a certain other person or with an animal; or

(2) That the act was done with a child under the age of 16; or

(3) That the act was done by force and without the consent of the other person.

<u>Explanation</u>. It is unnatural carnal copulation for a person to take into that person's mouth or anus the sexual organ of another person or of an animal; or to place that person's organ in the mouth or anus of another person or of an animal; or to have carnal copulation in any opening of the body, except the sexual parts, with another person; or to have carnal copulation with an animal.

<u>Maximum punishment</u>

(1) By force and without consent or with a child under the age of 16: Dishonorable discharge, total forfeiture of pay & allowances, fine, confinement at hard labor for 20 years

(2) Other cases: Dishonorable discharge, total forfeiture of pay & allowances, fine, confinement at hard labor for 5

A-4

Elements

    (1)   That the accused assaulted a certain person;

    (2)   That, at the time of the assault, the accused intended to commit sodomy; and

    (3)   That, under the circumstances, the conduct of the accused was to the prejudice of good order and discipline in the armed forces or was of a nature to bring discredit upon the armed forces.

Explanation. Assault with intent to commit sodomy is an assault against a human being and must be committed with a specific intent to commit sodomy. Any lesser intent, or different intent, will not suffice.

Maximum punishment

    (1)   Dishonorable discharge, total forfeiture of pay & allowances, fine, confinement at hard labor for 10 years

    (2)   Other cases: Dishonorable discharge, total forfeiture of pay & allowances, fine, confinement at hard labor for 5 years

A-5

Elements

    (1)   That the accused assaulted a certain person not the spouse of the accused in a certain manner;

    (2)   That the acts were done with the intent to gratify the lust or sexual desires of the accused; and

    (3)   That, under the circumstances, the conduct of the accused was to the prejudice of good order and discipline in the armed forces or was of a nature to bring discredit upon the armed forces.

Explanation. "Indecent" signifies that form of immorality relating to sexual impurity which is not only grossly vulgar, obscene, and repugnant to common propriety, but tends to excite lust and deprave the morals with respect to sexual relations.

Maximum punishment

    (1)   Dishonorable discharge, total forfeiture of pay & allowances, fine, confinement at hard labor for 5 years

A-6

Article 134 - Indecent Acts with Another

Elements

(1)   That the accused committed a certain wrongful
      act with a certain person;

(2)   That the act was indecent; and

(3)   That, under the circumstances, the conduct of
      the accused was to the prejudice of good order
      and discipline in the armed forces or was of a
      nature to bring discredit upon the armed forces.

Explanation. "Indecent" signifies that form of immorality relating to sexual impurity which is not only grossly vulgar, obscene, and repugnant to common propriety, but tends to excite lust and deprave the morals with respect to sexual relations.

Maximum punishment

(1)   Dishonorable discharge, total forfeiture of pay
      & allowances, fine, confinement at hard labor
      for 5 years

A-7

B. DoD Regulations

The DoD regulations covering separation from service of homosexual members consist of:

1. DoD Directive 1332.14

   Enlisted Administrative Separation

2. DoD Directive 1332.30

   Separation of Regular Commissioned Officers for Cause.

A-8

Homosexuality (Part 1, Section H)

1. Basis

    a.   Homosexuality is incompatible with military service. The presence in the military environment of persons who engage in homosexual conduct or who, by their statements, demonstrate a propensity to engage in homosexual conduct, seriously impairs the accomplishment of the military mission. The presence of such members adversely affects the ability of the Military Services to maintain discipline, good order, and morale; to foster mutual trust and confidence among servicemembers, to ensure the integrity of the system of rank and command; to facilitate assignment and worldwide deployment of servicemembers who frequently must live and work under close conditions affording minimal privacy; to recruit and retain members of the Military Services; to maintain the public acceptability of military service; and to prevent breaches of security.

    b.   As used in this action:

        (1)   Homosexual means a person, regardless of sex, who engages in, desires to engage in, or intends to engage in homosexual acts;

        (2)   Bisexual means a person who engages in, desires to engage in, or intends to engage in homosexual and heterosexual acts; and

        (3)   A homosexual act means bodily contact, actively undertaken or passively permitted, between members of the same sex for the purpose of satisfying sexual desires.

    c.   The basis for separation may include preservice, prior service, or current service conduct or statements. A member shall be separated under this section if one or more of the following approved findings is made:

        (1)   The member has engaged in, attempted to engage in, or solicited another to engage in a homosexual act or acts unless there are approved further findings that:

        (a)   Such conduct is a departure from the member's usual and customary behavior;

A-9

(b)   Such conduct under all the circumstances is unlikely to recur;

(c)   Such conduct was not accomplished by use of force, coercion, or intimidation by the member during a period of military service;

(d)   Under the particular circumstances of the case, the member's continued presence in the Service is consistent with the interest of the Service in proper discipline, good order, and morale; and

(e)   The member does not desire to engage in or intend to engage in homosexual acts.

(2)   The member has stated that he or she is a homosexual or bisexual unless there is a further finding that the member is not a homosexual or bisexual.

(3)   The member has married or attempted to marry a person known to be of the same biological sex (as evidenced by the external anatomy of the persons involved) unless there are further findings that the member is not a homosexual or bisexual and that the purpose of the marriage or attempt was the avoidance or termination of military service.

A-10

DEFINITIONS

Bisexual. A person who engages in, desires to engage in, or intends to engage in both homosexual and heterosexual acts.

Homosexual. A person, regardless of sex, who engages in, desires to engage in, or intends to engage in homosexual acts.

Homosexual Act. Bodily contact, actively undertaken or passively permitted, between members of the same sex for the purpose of satisfying sexual desires.

ACTS OF MISCONDUCT OR MORAL OR PROFESSIONAL DERELICTION

Homosexuality. The basis for separation may include preservice, prior service, or current service conduct or statements. A commissioned officer shall be separated under this provision if one or more of the following findings is made:

a. The officer has engaged in, has attempted to engage in, or has solicited another to engage in a homosexual act or acts, unless there are further findings that:

(1) Such conduct is a departure from the officer's usual and customary behavior;

(2) Such conduct under all the circumstances is unlikely to recur;

(3) Such conduct was not accomplished by use of force, coercion, or intimidation by the officer during a period of military service;

(4) Under the particular circumstances of the case, the officer's continued presence in the Service is consistent with the proper discipline, good order, and morale of the Service; and

(5) The officer does not desire to engage in or intend to engage in homosexual acts.

A-11

b.   The officer has stated that he or she is a homosexual or bisexual unless there is a **further** finding that the officer is not a homosexual or bisexual.

c.   The officer has married or attempted to marry a person known to be of the same biological sex (as evidenced by the external anatomy of the persons involved) unless there are further findings that the officer is not a homosexual or bisexual and that the purpose of the marriage or attempt was the avoidance or termination of military service.

CHARACTER OF DISCHARGE

A discharge shall be characterized as "Honorable" or "Under Honorable Conditions" when the sole basis for separation is homosexuality unless aggravated acts are included in the findings. A separation "Under Other Than Honorable Conditions" may be issued if there is a finding that the Service member attempted, solicited, or committed a homosexual act.

(1)   By using force, coercion, or intimidation.

(2)   With a person under 16 years of age.

(3)   With a subordinate in circumstances that violate the customary military superior-subordinate relationship.

(4)   Openly in public view.

(5)   For compensation.

(6)   Aboard a military vessel or aircraft.

(7)   In another location subject to military control under aggravating circumstances, noted in the finding, that have an adverse impact on discipline, good order, or morale comparable to the impact of such activity aboard a vessel or aircraft.

A-12

C. Service Regulations

The individual Service Regulations concerning homosexuality are as follows:

1. U.S. Army - U.S. Army Regulation 635-200

2. U.S. Navy - SECNAVINST 1900.9C (Policy for members of naval service involved in homosexual conduct.)

   - SECNAVINST 1920.4A (Enlisted Administrative Separations)

   - SECNAVINST 1920.6A (Administrative Separations of Officers)

   - NAVMILPERSCOMINS 1910.1C

   - MILPERSMAN 3630400 (Separation by reason of homosexuality)

3. U.S. Marine Corps
   - Marine Corps Separation and Retirement Manual, 1900-16C, paragraph 6207 (Officers & Enlisted)

4. U.S. Air Force
   - Air Force Regulation 39-10 (Administrative discharge of Airmen), Chapter 5, Section 6

   - Air Force Regulation 36-2 (Separation of Officers), Chapter 3, paragraph 4

5. U.S. Coast Guard - Personnel Manual Articles:

   - 12-B-16 discharge for unsuitability

   - 12-B-18 discharge for homosexuality

   - 12-B-33 discharge processing

The service regulations, although they differ somewhat in wording, substantially repeat the DoD regulations on which they are based. For that reason they are not reproduced here.

A-13

D. Security Regulations

The security clearance aspects of homosexuality (and other sexual behavior) are addressed by DoD 5200-2-R, the Department of Defense Personnel Security Program Regulation. This program covers military personnel, DoD civilians, and DoD contractor civilian employees, if they are submitted for a security clearance.

Security considerations are also addressed by the Director of Central Intelligence Directive No. 1/14 (DCID 1/14 of 14 April 1986) which gives the minimum personnel security standards governing eligibility for access to Sensitive Compartmented Information (SCI clearance). This applies to DoD clearances as well as all other security clearances of that level.

A-14

GAYS IN UNIFORM

EXTRACT FROM DEPARTMENT OF DEFENSE PERSONNEL SECURITY
PROGRAM REGULATION, DoD 5200.2-R - 16 Dec 1986

APPENDIX I

ADJUDICATION POLICY
GENERAL

The following adjudication policy has been developed to assist DoD adjudicators in making determinations with respect to an individual's eligiblity for employment or retention in sensitive duties or eligibility for access to classified informatlion. Adjudication policy relative to access to sensitive compartmented information is contained in DCID1/14.

While reasonable consistency in reaching adjudicative determinations is desirable, the nature and complexities of human behavior preclude the development of a single set of guidelines or policies that is equally applicable in every personnel security case. Accordingly, the following adjudication policy is not intended to be interpreted as inflexible rules of procedures. The following policy requires dependence on the adjudicator's sound judgment, mature thinking, and careful analysis as each case must be weighed on its own merits, taking into consideration all relevant circumstances, and prior experience in similar cases as well as the guidelines contained in the adjudication policy, which have been compiled from common experience in personnel security determinations.

Each adjudication is to be an overall common sense determination based upon consideration and assessment of all available information, both favorable and unfavorable, with particular emphasis being placed on the seriousness, recency, frequency and motivation for the individual's conduct; the extent to which conduct was negligent, willful, voluntary, or undertaken with knowledge of the circumstances or consequencesa involved; and, to the extent that it can be estimated, the probability that conduct will or will not continue in the future. The listed "Disqualifying Factors" and "Mitigating Factors" in this set of Adjudication Policies reflect the consideration of those factors of seriousness, recency, frequency, motivation, etc., to common situations and types of behavior encountered in personnel security adjudications, and should be followed whenever an individual case can be measured against this policy guidance. Common sense may occasionally necessitate deviations from this policy guidance; but such deviations should not be frequently made and must be carefully explained and documented.

The "Disqualifying Factors" provided herein establish some of the types of serious conduct under the criteria that can justify a determination to deny or revoke an individual's eligibility for access to classified information, or appointment to, or retention

A-15

in sensitive duties. The "Mitigating Factors" establish some of the types of circumstances that may mitigate the conduct listed under the "Disqualifying Factors." Any determination must include a consideration of both the conduct listed under "Disqualifying Factors" and any circumstances listed under the appropriate or corresponding "Mitigating Factors."

The adjudication policy is subdivided into sections appropriate to each of the criteria provided in paragraph 2-200 of this regulation, except 2-200.i., for which conduct under any of the "Disqualifying Factors" of the adjudication policy or any other types of conduct may be appropriately included, if it meets the definition of paragraph 2-200.i.

In all adjudications, the protection of the national security shall be the paramount determinant. In the last analysis, a final decision in each case must be arrived at by applying the standard that the issuance of the clearance or assignment to the sensitive position is "clearly consistent with the interests of national security."

SEXUAL MISCONDUCT

Basis: Acts of sexual misconduct or perversion indicative of moral turpitude, poor judgment, or lack of regard for the laws of society.

Disqualifying Factors (behavior falls within one or more of the following categories):

1.   The conduct involves:

   a.   Acts performed or committed in open or public places.

   b.   Acts performed with a minor, or with animals.

   c.   Acts involving inducement, coercion, force, violence or intimidation of another person.

   d.   Prostitution, pandering or the commission of sexual acts for money or other remuneration or reward.

   e.   Sexual harassment.

   f.   Self mutilation, self punishment or degradation.

   g.   Conduct that involves spouse swapping, or group sex orgies.

A-16

h.   Adultery that is recent, frequent and likely to continue and has an adverse effect on good order or discipline within the workplace (e.g., officer/enlisted, supervisor/ subordinate, instructor/student).

i.   Conduct determined to be criminal in the locale in which it occurred.

j.   Deviant or perverted sexual behavior which may indicate a mental or personality disorder (e.g., transexualism, transvestism, exhibitionism, incest, child molestation, voyeurism, bestiality, or sodomy).

2.   The conduct has been recent.

3.   The conduct increases the individual's vulnerability to blackmail, coercion or pressure.

4.   Evidence that the applicant has intention or is likely to repeat the conduct in question.

Mitigating Factors (circumstances which may mitigate qualifying information):

1.   Sexual misconduct occurred on an isolated basis during or preceding adolescence with no evidence of subsequent conduct or a similar nature, and clear indication that the individual has no intention of participating in such conduct in the future.

2.   Sexual misconduct was isolated, occurred more than 3 years ago, and there is clear indication that the individual has no intention of participating in such conduct in the future.

3.   The individual was a minor or was the victim of force, or violence by another.

4.   The individual has successfully completed professional therapy, has been rehabilitated and diagnosed by competent medical authority that misconduct is not likely to recur.

5.   Demonstration that the individual's sexual misconduct can no longer form the basis for vulnerability to blackmail, coercion or pressure.

A-17

ANNEX A

ADJUDICATION GUIDELINES

PURPOSE

This annex is designed to ensure that a common approach is followed by Intelligence Community departments and agencies in applying the standards of DCID 1/14. These guidelines apply to the adjudication of cases involving persons being considered for first-time access to Sensitive Compartmented Information (SCI) as well as those cases of persons being readjudicated for continued SCI access.

ADJUDICATIVE PROCESS

The adjudicative process entails the examination of a sufficient period of a man's life to make a determination that the person is not now or is not likely to become an unacceptable security risk later. SCI access adjudication is the careful weighing of a number of variables known as the "whole person" concept. The recency of occurrence of any adverse incident, together with circumstances pertaining thereto, is central to a fair and uniform evaluation. Key factors to be considered in adjudication are the maturity and responsibility of the person at the time certain acts or violations were committed as well as any repetition or continuation of such conduct. Each case must be judged on its own merits and final determination remains the responsibility of the individual SOIC. Any doubt concerning personnel having access to SCI shall be resolved in favor of the national security.

The ultimate determination of whether the granting of SCI access is clearly consistent with the interests of national security shall be an overall common sense determination based on all available information. In arriving at a decision consistent with the foregoing, the adjudicator must give careful scrutiny to the following matters:

a. Loyalty

b. Close relatives and associates

c. Sexual considerations

d. Cohabitation

e. Undesirable character traits

f. Financial irresponsibility

A-18

g.   Alcohol abuse

h.   Illegal drugs and drug abuse

i.   Emotional and mental disorders

j.   Record of law violations

k.   Security violations

l.   Involvement in outside activities

Adjudicative actions concerning the foregoing items are examined in greater detail below.

SEXUAL CONSIDERATIONS

DCID 1/14 requires that, to be eligible for SCI access, individuals must be stable, of excellent character and discretion, and not subject to undue influence or duress through exploitable personal conduct.

Sexual promiscuity, prostitution, and extramarital relations are of legitimate concern to the SCI adjudicator where such conduct reflects a lack of judgment and discretion or when the conduct offers the potential for undue influence, duress or exploitation by a foreign intelligence service.

Deviant sexual behavior can be a relevant consideration in circumstances in which it indicates flawed judgment or a personality disorder, or could result in exposing the individual to direct or indirect pressure because of susceptibility to blackmail or coercion as a result of the deviant sexual behavior. Such behavior includes, but is not limited to, bestiality, fetishism, exhibitionism, necrophilia, nymphomania or satyriasis, masochism, sadism, pedophilia, transvestism, and voyeurism. Homosexual conduct is also to be considered as a factor in determining an individual's judgment, discretion, stability and susceptibility to undue influence or duress.

In examining cases involving sexual conduct of security significance, such as those described above, it is relevant to consider the age of the person, the voluntariness, and the frequency of such activities, the public nature and the recency of the conduct, as well as any other circumstances which may serve to aggravate or mitigate the nature or character of the conduct. A recommendation for disapproval is appropriate when, in view of all available evidence concerning the individual's history of sexual behavior, it appears that access to SCI could pose a risk to the national security.

A-19

II. Current Civilian Criminal Law

A. Overview

The most notable landmark in Western policy toward homosexuals is probably the Wolfenden Report. In 1954 the British government appointed a commission chaired by J. F. Wolfenden to consider the law and practice with regard to homosexual offenses and prostitution. The Committee published its findings in 1957 (The Wolfenden Report, 1963). It recommended (among other things) that homosexual behavior between consenting adults in private should no longer be a criminal offense. This recommendation was implemented for the most part in England in 1967 by the Sexual Offenses Act (Rosen, 1979).

Rosen points out that in England, in spite of reforms, the law remains complicated with regard to sexual offenses. Although English law does not forbid "private consenting adult (over 21) homosexual behavior" with regard to buggery (anal intercourse) or gross indecency (which is not defined), this applies only in England and Wales. Anal intercourse among heterosexuals, even if married, remains a crime throughout Britain. The cited homosexual acts continue to be illegal in Scotland, Northern Ireland and in the British Armed Forces and the Merchant Marine. With regard to female homosexual acts, Rosen states that "lesbianism has never been a crime in England, nor anywhere else so far as is known."[*]

There have been general movements toward liberalization of such laws, especially in western Europe, in the Scandinavian countries and in West Germany. The Ninth International Congress on Criminal law and in the U.S., the American Law Institute in its Model Penal Code of 1955 recommended the decriminalization of private homosexual acts between consenting adults (Livingood, 1976). In Canadian law, consenting adult homosexual acts were prosecutable until 1967 (Zuliani, 1986).

Homosexual behavior was not considered a criminal offense in the U.S.S.R. after the revolution of 1917. In 1934 it was made a felony. The U.S.S.R. criminal code makes no mention of female homosexuality (Brzek & Hubalek, 1988). Homosexual behavior is also a criminal offense in Rumania. The other European communist countries are more liberal, and generally criminalize homosexual behavior only when other offenses such as contact with a minor are involved. In all of the communist countries there are apparently no official instructions against the employment of homosexuals except in the police and the military.

---

[*]Most American sodomy laws extend prohibitions to "all persons," "any persons," and "any human being," but actual prosecutions of females under these laws is rare.

A-20

The laws of the German Democratic Republic towards homosexuals are the most liberal of the communist bloc. In spite of the extremely tolerant official attitude toward homosexuality, employing homosexuals in the police force or army of the GDR is not under consideration (Brzek & Hubalek, 1988).

B. U.S. State Criminal Law

The first U.S. state to decriminalize adult homosexual activities was Illinois in 1962. At that time each of the other 49 states had sodomy laws on the books. Forty-five also penalized adultery, 37 states penalized fornication and 15 states penalized cohabitation. Hefner (1964) noted that even though Illinois had decriminalized consenting adult sodomy it retained laws against adultery and fornication, creating the curious situation of permitting certain "homosexual (and other) perversions" while prohibiting some "normal" heterosexual activities. Hefner observed, "We are free in a voting booth, in a stockholders' meeting, a union hall or a house of worship, but we are not free in bed."

The next six states to join Illinois in removing criminal laws against private consenting adult homosexual acts were Colorado, Delaware, Oregon, Hawaii and Ohio (Geis et al, 1976). By 1977, homosexuality was illegal between consenting adults in only 31 states (Bell & Weinberg, 1978). Currently (1988) there are no so-called sodomy laws in 25 states. Adult consenting homosexual behavior is legal in:

Alaska	Illinois
Hawaii	Indiana
California	Oklahoma
Oregon	West Virginia
Washington	Pennsylvania
Wyoming	New York
Colorado	Delaware
New Mexico	New Jersey
Nebraska	Connecticut
South Dakota	Vermont
North Dakota	New Hampshire
Iowa	Maine
Wisconsin	

Clearly the trend is toward liberalization of the law.

In 25 states and the District of Columbia, however, sodomy laws remain in force. In some of these, such as Texas, Arkansas, Kansas, Montana and Nevada, homosexual acts between males are specified for prohibition. In most other state laws, sodomy is

A-21

spoken of in broader terms as "crimes against nature" and can be applied equally to heterosexual behavior. Generally, such sodomy laws make no distinction between married and unmarried partners.

Along with liberalized laws in half of the states, there is apparently a high level of de facto acceptance of homosexuality throughout the U.S. Most large cities have recognized homosexual areas and bars. Some cities such as New Orleans and Key West are well known "homosexual centers" in spite of being located in states where sodomy laws remain in force.*

It is important to remember that the term, "sodomy," does not always have a standard meaning, either in common usage or in law.

The Random House College Dictionary (U.S. Government Edition), commonly used in government offices, gives the following definition:

1. unnatural, especially anal copulation

2. copulation of a human with an animal, bestiality (the word is derived from Sodom, a Biblical city referred to in Genesis 18-19, which was destroyed by God because of its wickedness.)

In California law, sodomy is "sexual conduct consisting of contact between the penis of one person and the anus of another person" (California Penal Code #285 note 24.5).

The term, sodomy, can be applied to anal intercourse, oral-genital contact, sexual contact with an animal, or any "unnatural copulation," whatever that may be. It certainly seems possible to apply this term to any of the less usual heterosexual positions of intercourse. In some cases even "heavy petting," such as hand-genital contact, can meet the legal definition of sodomy. Marriage of the partners seems to offer no immunity from prosecution for such acts.

Other terms for illegal intercourse which are sometimes encountered are buggery and pederasty. Both of these imply anal intercourse. Pederasty usually refers to anal intercourse between an adult and a male minor. It is derived from a Greek word which means "lover of boys." The word buggery has an interesting derivation from the Middle English word "bougre" or "bolgre" which meant heretic. The significance of this linguistic development was described on page 13.

---

*The penalty for sodomy in Florida is 20 years imprisonment.

A-22

GAYS IN UNIFORM

As has been pointed out, the UCMJ Article 125 definition of sodomy is particularly broad and covers homosexual acts as well as heterosexual acts even within marriage. Theoretically a large percentage of DoD military personnel might be criminals under it. In practice, it is used almost exclusively to punish acts which involve force and/or a minor or nonconsenting partner. The larger percentage of such prosecuted acts are heterosexual.

C. U.S. Federal Criminal Law

With the exception of the UCMJ and certain laws pertaining to Indian reservations, Federal law does not proscribe homosexual behavior.

A-23

APPENDIX B

Military Service Separation
for Homosexuality

B-0

Military Service Separation
for Homosexuality

Data are given for Fiscal Year 85, 86 & 87 separations for homosexuality for all four of the DoD military services.* It is difficult to compare these data to those of earlier years, such as those reported in the Williams and Weinberg study (1971), because of differences in methods of recording and reporting data. Williams and Weinberg were unable to get exact data on the numbers and types of discharges for homosexuality for any of the armed services. It does appear that the total number of discharges for reasons of homosexuality and other sexual deviations may have decreased, and there is a remarkable decrease in the number of punitive discharges for homosexuality for all services.

*John Goral, Defense Manpower Data Center, 1988, unpublished data.

B-1

U.S. Army Discharges for Homosexuality

		FY 85		FY 86		FY 87	
		M	F	M	F	M	F
Enlisted Personnel	(E)	598,579	67,980	597,516	69,153	597,278	71,133
Officer Personnel	(O)	99,189	10,828	98,821	11,263	96,690	11,569
Administrative	E	234	110	353	137	242	107
Separations	O	3	0	2	3	6	0
Courts Martial	E	0	0	0	0	0	0
Separations	O	0	0	0	0	0	0
Total Homosexual	E	234	110	353	137	242	107
Separations	O	3	0	2	3	6	0
% Personnel	E	0.04	0.16	0.06	0.20	0.04	0.15
Separated	O	0.003	0	0.002	0.026	0.006	0
Number of CID	E						
Investigations	O						

*Army CID does not keep statistics by fiscal year or by homosexuality investigations. Records are maintained by offense code: i.e., sodomy, indecent acts, etc.

U.S. Navy Discharges for Homosexuality

		FY 85		FY 86		FY 87	
		M	F	M	F	M	F
Enlisted Personnel	(E)	462,223	45,328	472,847	46,796	480,926	47,328
Officer Personnel	(O)	65,379	6,991	66,602	7,370	66,736	7,379
Administrative	E	653	134	621	144	550	104
Separations	O	11	1	12	1	7	2
Courts Martial	E	1	0	0	0	0	0
Separations	O	1	0	0	0	0	0
Total Homosexual	E	654	134	621	144	550	104
Separations	O	12	1	12	1	7	2
% Personnel	E	0.14	0.30	0.13	0.30	0.11	0.22
Separated	O	0.02	0.01	0.02	0.01	0.01	0.03
Number of NIS	E	862	283	803	241	522	118
Investigations	O	41	10	32	6	33	3

B-2

GAYS IN UNIFORM

U.S. Marine Corps Discharges for Homosexuality

		FY 85		FY 86		FY 87	
		M	F	M	F	M	F
Enlisted Personnel (E)		168,809	9,041	169,369	9,246	170,338	9,140
Officer Personnel (O)		19,521	654	19,556	643	19,398	649
Administrative	E	87	33	59	26	67	31
Separations	O	2	0	2	0	2	0
Courts Martial	E	0	0	0	0	0	0
Separations	O	0	0	0	0	0	0
Total Homosexual	E	87	33	59	26	67	31
Separations	O	2	0	2	0	2	0
% Personnel	E	0.05	0.37	0.03	0.28	0.04	0.34
Separated	O	0.01	0	0.01	0	0.01	0
Number of NIS	E	177	77	120	84	137	47
Investigations	O	1	4	4	2	7	2

U.S. Air Force Discharges for Homosexuality

		FY 85		FY 86		FY 87	
		M	F	M	F	M	F
Enlisted Personnel (E)		431,017	57,586	433,972	60,694	432,578	62,666
Officer Personnel (O)		96,473	11,927	96,671	12,377	95,013	12,665
Administrative	E	201	81	249	68	194	71
Separations	O	15	3	13	2	13	2
Courts Martial	E	0	0	0	0	0	0
Separations	O	0	0	0	0	0	0
Total Homosexual	E	201	81	249	68	194	71
Separations	O	15	3	13	2	13	2
% Personnel	E	0.04	0.10	0.05	0.10	0.04	0.10
Separated	O	0.01	0.02	0.01	0.02	0.01	0.02
Number of OSI	E	177	80	132	51	142	52
Investigations	O	15	4	21	7	20	5

B-3

Williams and Weinberg (1971), in discussing discharges for the 1950s and 60s had already noted these trends in all of the armed services. They also noted that the Navy discharges a higher percentage of officers for homosexuality than do the other services. This trend is still in existence to the present, with the Navy discharging a higher percentage of both officers and enlisted men for homosexuality.

The overall discharge rate for homosexuality as reported in 1971 (Williams and Weinberg, 1971) as an estimate of "less than 1/10 of 1%," i.e. 0.001. The averaged discharge rates for the three fiscal years (85, 86, 87) cited in this report are somewhat greater:

Army	0.05% for enlisted men
	0.17% for enlisted women
	0.004% for male officers
	0.007% for female officers
Navy	0.13% for enlisted men
	0.27% for enlisted women
	0.02% for male officers
	0.02% for female officers
Marine	0.040% for enlisted men
	0.33% for enlisted women
	0.01% for male officers
	0 % for female officers
Air Force	0.043% for enlisted men
	0.1% for enlisted women
	0.01% for male officers
	0.02% for female officers

These data point to the conclusion that the percentage of people discharged for homosexuality (number of discharges for homosexuality divided by total personnel x 100) has actually increased.

B-4

APPENDIX C
Statistical Data on Homosexuality

C-0

Statistical Data on Homosexuality

No one knows how many homosexuals there are. The reason for this is twofold. First, there is the problem of definition, which has been discussed in the text. While it is relatively simple to define a homosexual act, it is not so with the definition of a homosexual person. Most definitions include some aspect of preference for or indulgence in homosexual acts. But how much preference, and how many acts? Along with authorities on human sexuality, we categorically reject the notion that participation in a single homosexual act defines homosexuality. An acceptable definition of homosexuality needs to contain two elements, one behavioral, the other self-definitional.

1. The person concerned prefers homosexual acts exclusively or significantly over heterosexual acts.

2. The person concerned identifies (at least privately) with being homosexual.

Second is the problem of locating homosexuals. Save for those who publicly announce their sexual orientation and those who are occasionally apprehended for homosexual conduct, there is no way to conduct population studies. Because of the social stigma traditionally attached to being homosexual, many (perhaps most) homosexuals remain hidden and are not identified except in special research studies. As a result, the data cited in any research investigation are not true population estimates. We can only construct estimates based on available data and social and demographic theory.

Kinsey (1948) rated his subjects on a 0-1-2-3-4-5-6 scale (which was described on page #638*) from exclusively heterosexual (0) to exclusively homosexual (6). Some of Kinsey's significant conclusions with regard to homosexuality are summarized in the following table:

---

*and in Appendix D. p. D-2.

C-1

Table 1

Heterosexual-Homosexual Ratings for all White Males

Heterosexual-Homosexual Rating: Active Incidence
(Total Population--U.S. Corrections)

Age	Cases	X	0	1	2	3	4	5	6
		%	%	%	%	%	%	%	%
5	4297	90.6	4.2	0.2	0.3	1.2	0.3	0.2	3.0
10	4296	61.1	10.8	1.7	3.6	5.6	1.3	0.5	15.4
15	4284	23.6	48.4	3.6	6.0	4.7	3.7	2.6	7.4
20	3467	3.3	69.3	4.4	7.4	4.4	2.9	3.4	4.9
25	1835	1.0	79.2	3.9	5.1	3.2	2.4	2.3	2.9
30	1192	0.5	83.1	4.0	3.4	2.1	3.0	1.3	2.6
35	844	0.4	86.7	2.4	3.4	1.9	1.7	0.9	2.6
40	576	1.3	86.8	3.0	3.6	2.0	0.7	0.3	2.3
45	382	2.7	88.8	2.3	2.0	1.3	0.9	0.2	1.8

Note: These are active incidence figures for the entire white male population, including single, married, and post-marital histories, the final figure corrected for the distribution of the population in the U.S. Census of 1940.

(from Kinsey, Pomeroy, Martin: Sexual Behavior in the Human Male, 1948).

With regard to how those data compare with data of other investigators, they state:

> it is useless to compare the 2 or 3 percent figure of Havelock Ellis, or the 2 to 5 percent figure of Hirschfeld, or the 0.1 per cent figure of the Army induction centers with any of the data given above. The persons who are identified as "homosexuals" in much of the legal and social practice have rated anything between 1 and 6 on the above scale. On the other hand, there are some persons who would not rate an individual as "really homosexual" if he were anything less than a 5 or 6. Nevertheless, it should be emphasized again that

C-2

there are persons who rate 2's or 3's who, in terms of the number of contacts they have made, may have had more homosexual experience than many persons who rate 6, and the clinician, the social worker, court officials, and society in general are not infrequently concerned with persons who rate no more than 2's or 3's. Many who rate only 1 or 2 are much disturbed over their homosexual experience, and they are frequently among those who go to clinicians for help.

With regard to bisexuality, Kinsey stated that nearly 46 percent of the general population engages in homosexual conduct or reacts to persons of both sexes in the course of their adult life.

Kinsey's data can be confusing, especially with regard to specific rates, because he excludes pre-adolescent homosexual experiences from many of his conclusions and presents such a wealth of numbers. The following conclusions, however, stand out:

- Only 50 percent of the population is exclusively heterosexual throughout adult life.

- Only 4 percent of the population is exclusively homosexual throughout adult life.

- Of the white male population, 10 percent is _more_ _or_ _less_ exclusively homosexual between ages 16 and 65.

- Throughout adult life, 46 percent have some homosexual contact.

The Kinsey data are complicated, largely due to the fact that sexual behavior patterns are not fixed, but change with age. This is probably best reflected by the following two graphs, also taken from Kinsey's work:

C-3

Heterosexual-homosexual ratings in total male population
(single and married) in any single year

```
Figure missing from
original report
```

Based on U.S. corrected data. Passing experiences eliminated from data by showing only ratings which have involved a period of at least three years after the males turned 16. Percent shown as "X" have virtually no socio-sexual contacts or reactions.

Development of Heterosexuality and Homosexuality
by Age Periods

```
Figure missing from
original report
```

Active incidence curves, corrected for U.S. population. Males with no socio-sexual response (rating X) rapidly disappear between the ages of 5 and 20. Males whose responses are chiefly heterosexual (rating 0 or 1) rapidly increase in number until they ultimately account for 90 per cent of the whole population. Males who are more than incidentally homosexual in response or overt activity (ratings 2-6) are most abundant in pre-adolescence and through the teens, gradually becoming less abundant with advancing age.

C-4

No study since Kinsey has been as comprehensive or thorough, and most subsequent work leans strongly on that of Kinsey.

The Wolfenden report (1957) also cites Kinsey's conclusions and states that findings in Great Britain might be similar. The Wolfenden report also alludes to data from Sweden concluding that 1 percent of all men were exclusively homosexual, and 4 percent had both homosexual and heterosexual impulses.

The Canadian Forces Study on Homosexuality (Zuliani, 1986) stated that 10 percent of the general Canadian population was "non-exclusively heterosexual." This study also estimated that 10 percent of males and 5 percent of females in the general population were exclusively homosexual for at least 3 years between ages 16 and 55. Williams and Weinberg (1971) do not give any estimates of total numbers of homosexuals in the military, but state "...there must be a considerable number of homosexuals. At the least, this number must be greater than the 2000-3000 discharges per year for homosexuality" (p. 59).

In the data reported by Harry (1984), homosexual men and heterosexual men seem equally likely to have served in the military. Lesbians are _more_ likely to have served than heterosexual women.

No hard data have been advanced to counter the conclusion that the percentage of male homosexuals in the military is significantly different from that in the general population. On the data available it is reasonable to conclude that the percentage of female homosexuality in the military is higher than in the general population.

C-5

APPENDIX D

Bisexuality

D-0

Bisexuality

The ancient Greek concept of organic bisexuality was revived with the science of embryology and the apparent early hermaphroditic characteristics of the human embryo (Marmor, 1975). Freud used this concept in formulating some of his psychoanalytic theories, and believed that there is a biologic bisexual predisposition, and that all persons go through a homoerotic phase as part of normal maturation.

Up to now there has been little consideration of bisexuality as a possible separate category. Bisexuality, that is erotic response to both sexes, has been generally included with homosexuality. This becomes clear if one considers most laws and rules concerning homosexual behavior: participation in a single homosexual act is enough to label a person a homosexual (Kinsey, 1948). The converse, however, is not true; a homosexual does not become heterosexual by engaging in sexual behavior with the opposite sex.

The Kinsey data, that 4 percent of men are exclusively homosexual, and 63 percent are exclusively heterosexual (after adolescence) leaves a very large percentage, .33 percent, who could be considered bisexual, as they exhibit varying degrees of erotic response to either sex.

D-1

```
┌─────────────────────────────┐
│                             │
│      Figure missing from    │
│       original report       │
│                             │
└─────────────────────────────┘
```

Heterosexual-homosexual rating scale

Based on both psychologic reactions and overt experience, individuals rate as follows:

0. Exclusively heterosexual with no homosexual
1. Predominantly heterosexual, only incidentally homosexual
2. Predominantly heterosexual, but more than incidentally homosexual
3. Equally heterosexual and homosexual
4. Predominantly homosexual, but more than incidentally heterosexual
5. Predominantly homosexual, but incidentally heterosexual
6. Exclusively homosexual

According to the Kinsey rating of 0 to 6, persons rated (1) through (5) can be labelled bisexual. Some have confined this label only to those identified as "3", which means "equally heterosexual and homosexual" (Kinsey, 1948). This, however, seems too restrictive, and the recent trend is to broaden the definition of bisexuality to "sexual, emotional and social attraction to both sexes" (Paul, 1984). If one accepts such a definition (which seems reasonable) then bisexuality encompasses Kinsey's ratings 1-5, and there are clearly more bisexuals than homosexuals. This has been pointed out by MacDonald (1982) who also states that researchers tend to include large numbers of bisexuals in the homosexual category, which leads him to question the validity of their conclusions.

Certainly there has been little research to date on bisexuality as a separate category, but there is increasing awareness of its possible significance among scientists as well as among homosexuals themselves (Klein and Wolf, 1985).

D-2

GAYS IN UNIFORM

In terms of military discharges for homosexuality, it seems likely that many of those individuals discharged as homosexuals are probably bisexual (and could be completely heterosexual except for one incident).

At present this issue is not addressed in military law or regulations. No distinction is made between homosexuality and bisexuality.

The bisexual capability exists in a large percentage of persons (perhaps 37 percent of males or more) and is probably the explanation for much of such "situational homosexuality" as is seen in prisons and other restricted environments where there is no access to members of the opposite sex. In most cases, persons participating in homosexual acts under such circumstances do not consider themselves homosexual, and return to heterosexual behavior when this becomes possible.

D-3

Part 2: The Memoranda

POLICY

1 8 JAN 1989

MEMORANDUM FOR DIRECTOR DOD PERSONNEL SECURITY RESEARCH AND
             EDUCATION CENTER

SUBJECT: PERS-TR-89-002, "Nonconforming Sexual Orientations
          and Military Suitability"

      We, together with other DoD staff elements, have reviewed
subject draft study and believe you missed the target. More-
over, you exceeded your authority by extending the research
effort beyond the personnel security arena, and into another
area entirely, namely suitability for military service.

      Wholly aside from PERSEREC's lack of authority to conduct
research into the military suitability area, we found PERS-TR-89-
002 to be technically flawed, to contain subject matter (Judeo-
Christian precepts) which has no place in a Department of Defense
publication, to reflect significant omissions with respect to
relevant court decisions concerning personnel security, and to
suggest a bias which does justice neither to PERSEREC nor the
Department.

      There is an immediate and important need to conduct research
in the personnel security area. I want you to concentrate on
that need. You are advised to carefully review the directions set
forth in my memorandum, subject: Initial Research Plan, dated 13
June 1986, addressed to the Director, Personnel Security Research
and Education Center (Attachment 1). You will find that your
authority to conduct initial research in the sexual misconduct
area is rather narrowly set forth in TAB 2-1, item 19, of the
Initial Research Plan. We supplemented this direction to you by
means of the Assistant Deputy Under Secretary of Defense (Counter-
intelligence and Security) memorandum, subject: PERSEREC and
Homosexuality Research, dated 26 October 1987 (Attachment 2).
You should review these two documents carefully. I want you to
renew your effort to develop a positive response to this latter
memorandum. In this connection, you should work closely with
Mr. Anderson's staff.

      With respect to other ongoing research, you must concentrate
on Priority I tasks as I directed in my 13 June 1986 memorandum.

Additionally, please identify any ongoing research efforts which I have not approved in writing, other than support requested by the Marine Security Guard Battalion, and provide me with a copy of the existing Statement of Work in each instance, together with your rationale as to why these efforts should not be discontinued in favor of the approved Priority I tasks.

You will note that in my 13 June 1986 memorandum, I directed you to coordinate with my office before any Priority II or other research efforts were pursued. I have been advised that some of your efforts and resources are being devoted, on a top priority basis, to "Prescreening for Security Positions." I have never specifically approved "Prescreening" as a Priority I research topic. We do not believe it is worth the effort. Accordingly, please submit by 31 January 1989 a schedule for an orderly, but early, termination of the "Prescreening" research (except for that already underway in support of the Marine Guard Force). If, at a later date, it is determined that "Prescreening" research should be re-initiated, you will be advised.

Lastly, I must ask that you coordinate in advance, as well as seek appropriate guidance, prior to initiating any PERSEREC research in areas which are questionable or have not been approved by my office. All of us want PERSEREC to succeed. The key to success is to ensure that materials are produced which are relevant, useful, and timely.

Craig Alderman, Jr.
Deputy

Attachments
As Stated

DEFENSE PERSONNEL SECURITY RESEARCH AND EDUCATION CENTER (PERSEREC)
99 PACIFIC STREET, BUILDING 455, SUITE E
MONTEREY, CALIFORNIA 93940-2481

65CE/0773DOD
30 January 1989

MEMORANDUM FOR THE DEPUTY UNDERSECRETARY OF DEFENSE (POLICY)

Subj: PERSEREC RESEARCH ON HOMOSEXUALITY AND SUITABILITY

Ref: (a) DUSD(P) memo to PERSEREC of 18 January 1989
           regarding PERS-TR-89-002

Encl: (1) Review of OSD guidance and PERSEREC's involvement
           in homosexuality research projects
       (2) Description of the two active PERSEREC projects
       (3) Description of the genesis of PERSEREC prescreening
           research

1. PERSEREC will comply fully with the guidance provided in
reference (a). I accept complete responsibility for not meeting
your expectations in the conduct of this research.

2. As directed by reference (a), enclosure 1 provides a detailed
review of the OSD guidance and our involvement in research
projects on homosexuality. Enclosure 2 is a description of the
only two active projects that are non-priority 1, with specific
recommendations for each. The statements of work issued to
contractors and currently in force are also provided. Enclosure
3 describes the genesis of PERSEREC prescreening research and
includes a schedule for terminating all prescreening activity.

3. I look forward to establishing a close and cooperative
working relationship with the new OSD security research coor-
dinator.

Carson K. Eoyang

CARSON K. EOYANG
Director

Review of Guidance on Homosexuality Research

1. __13 June 1986__   DUSD(P) approved ten top priority research areas including I-2: "Validate existing criteria for personnel security clearance determinations, and develop more objective, uniform, and valid adjudication standards, e.g., develop nexus with respect to the various criteria.

Question 19: Can we rationalize the disposition of the cases of individuals who have committed adultery and the disposition of the cases of homosexuals in the adjudicative process? Likewise, the cases of individuals who abuse alcohol and the cases of those who abuse drugs?"

2. __2 Sept 1987__   PERSEREC received from Mr. William Fedor a copy of a letter from DEPSECDEF to Congresswoman Schroeder (dated 19 Aug 1987) that read in part:

"As you may know, the basic DoD personnel security adjudicative guidelines were initially issued in December 1979, long before the establishment of the DoD Personnel Security Research and Education Center (PERSEREC). The January 1987 revision clarifies the guidelines but does not fundamentally change them. In 1986, immediately after the establishment of PERSEREC, we initiated personnel security research relating to the issues you raise in your June 15, 1987 letter. The pace of such research is, of course, affected by the relatively small number of espionage cases or security compromises providing the basis of analysis. We believe that it is prudent and appropriate to base our personnel security determinations upon the existing guidelines, until substantive evidence is developed through research, or other means, that our approach is invalid.

We shall continue to press, as time and resources permit, for early development of quality research products addressing these matters."

PERSEREC also received copies of letters and memos sent to DoD, FBI, and CIA requesting they identify "real world" espionage cases where homosexuality was a factor. Also appended was the deposition that J. F. Donnelly gave in the High Tech Gays case.

3. __28 Sept 1987__   PERSEREC forwarded to ADUSD four documents relating to research on homosexuality. One was a technical note by Dr. Michael McDaniel on homosexuality and pre-service adjustment factors. The second was a Naval Postgraduate School thesis on homosexuality and the military. The third was a journal article reviewing the origins of sexual preference. The fourth was an analysis of the Armed Services Adaptability Profile (ASAP) with respect to homosexuals.

Five alternative research topics were outlined and submitted for guidance.

4. <u>26 Oct 1987</u>   ADUSD(CI&S) memo to PERSEREC responded to our
28 Sept memo by providing amplifying guidance. The materials
that were sent were regarded as "somewhat off the target".
Comparisons of homosexual and heterosexuals with regard to job
performance were discouraged as was use of information from the
"American Psychological Association, or adherents to its general
approach concerning homosexuality".

PERSEREC's attention was directed to the following statement: "The governing factors, generally speaking, with respect to
sexual misconduct are whether a particular individual has engaged
or engages in acts which are criminal, notoriously disgraceful,
reckless or irresponsible, constitute sexual perversion, or
indicate lack of judgment or stability. It is also relevant
whether the particular conduct is criminal in the jurisdiction in
which the subject resides (which sodomy is in many States), the
extent to which it involves minors, and whether it is indicative
of instability or lack of good judgment, together with considerations of whether in the given case the individual is vulnerable
to blackmail or otherwise may be coerced so as to act contrary to
the national interest."

5. <u>19 Nov 1987</u>   Pursuant to 26 October 1987 memo, Dr.
McDaniel met with CPT Dale Stalf, Office of DoD General Counsel
to review documentation collected by Mr. Fedor's office. They
both agreed that the evidence was inconclusive and inappropriate
for scientific research. CPT Stalf requested <u>all</u> information
that was relevant to homosexuals and not just that which is
supportive of DoD policy. Later that day CPT Stalf called Dr.
Eoyang to reiterate that OSD was not directing PERSEREC to arrive
at predetermined conclusions and that he wanted all materials
that bear on the subject, especially information that pertained
to homosexuals' trustworthiness, reliability, or vulnerability to
blackmail.

6. <u>11 Dec 1987</u>   Mr. William Fedor and Mr. Peter Nelson met
with Dr. McDaniel and CAPT Kenneth Karols to review homosexual
research under development. Preliminary data regarding homosexuals and pre-service suitability were discussed. Mr. Fedor
discouraged the pursuit of this particular line of analysis and
redirected Dr. McDaniel to consult the collection of homosexual
espionage anecdotes in support of DoD policy.

7. <u>22 June 1988</u>   Panel discussion, "Sexual Nexus Round Table:
Sexual Misconduct" was held during the Personnel Security
Research Symposium held at the Naval Postgraduate School. The
panelists included:

     Mr. Maurice E. White, Esq., Senior Attorney Advisor, Office
of Legal Counsel, Department of Defense
     Mr. Allan Adler, Esq., Legislative Counsel for the Center
for National Security Studies, American Civil Liberties Union

2

Major Richard Bloom, Ph.D., Joint Chiefs of Staff
   Mr. Andrew A. Feinstein, Esq., Staff Director, Subcommittee
on Civil Service, U.S. House of Representatives
   Mrs. Bette Lyons, Chief, Adjudicators Division, Army Central
Clearance Facility
   Ms. Barbara Knox, Chief, Investigative Policy Division,
Defense Investigative Service.

The presentations and discussion were substantive, wide ranging
and illuminating. Only papers by Maj. Bloom and Mr. Feinstein
were available for inclusion in the published symposium proceed-
ings.

8. 28 Sept 1988   Director (CI&SP) memo to PERSEREC requested
status of progress on developing materials requested by
ADUSD(CI&S) memo of 26 October 1987.

9. 13 Oct 1988   PERSEREC memo to Director (CI&S) outlined
progress made since 27 Sept 1987. Specifically the memo stated:

"In the past year, PERSEREC has pursued two independent
lines of inquiry relevant to the issue of homosexuality. First
Ted Sarbin and Ken Karols have been undertaking a comprehensive
review of the scientific literature on the suitability and
reliability of individuals with nonconforming sexual orientations. This is an attempt to place homosexuality in a larger
context of sexual behavior in general and to examine the available evidence on vulnerabilities. The latest draft of this
report should be available for security review by OSD sometime in
November.

The second approach is to review unclassified information on
all known American espionage cases to determine the number of
instances in which homosexuality figured prominently in the
commission of the crimes."

10. 15 Dec 1988   A working draft of "Nonconforming Sexual
Orientations and Military Suitability" by T. Sarbin and K. Karols
was submitted to the Director (CI&SP) for preliminary review.
Dr. Sarbin (a distinguished psychologist from the University of
California) and CAPT Karols (a Navy flight surgeon and board
certified psychiatrist) were selected for this assignment for
their expert qualifications in research and military medicine.

11. 18 Jan 1989   DUSD(P) memo to PERSEREC critically reviewed
subject draft report and directed closer adherence to OSD guidance previously provided.

In summary, PERSEREC has throughout attempted to respond
faithfully to the direction provided regarding this research
area. Our intention in undertaking the subject report was to
address directly the "governing factors" specified in the

3

ADUSD(CI&S) memo of 26 October 1987. The paper does indeed
examine nonconforming sexual behaviors in terms of their crimi-
nality, notoriety, recklessness, and perversion in a dynamic
society in which customs, mores, and laws are in rapid transition. It does not address the full policy, legal, and political
ramifications which are properly the province of other offices in
DoD.

It is our contention that if the study had concluded that
there was unequivocal scientific evidence that homosexuals were
demonstrably unsuitable and unreliable, then by logical inference
such individuals would per force be inappropriate candidates for
critical and sensitive positions requiring security clearances.
Indeed, had the study results turned out affirmatively, it is
likely that these efforts would have been quite instrumental in
defending and strengthening current policy. Although the
Sarbin/Karols draft did not corroborate this particular conclusion, this was not known until the completion of the study.
The nature of research is such that the answers to the focal
question are not known in advance. The underlying purpose for
asking the question should not be invalidated because the results
turn out to be problematic from a policy perspective.

Although we recognized the inconsistencies between the
implications of the study and current DoD policy, the draft
report was forwarded to OSD for review and comment, in the hope
that a frank and quiet examination of the issues could be conducted within our immediate chain of command. In conformance
with the Office of General Counsel's admonition to furnish all
relevant information, the report was submitted to the Director
(CI&SP) for internal review only, to be used by OSD as it sees
fit. The alternative of completely suppressing the report within
PERSEREC without explicit guidance was rejected as presumptuous
and irresponsible.

We have invoked the tightest controls on the reproduction of
and access to all copies. Except for the three copies sent to
Mr. Pollari for security review, all our copies are accounted for
and kept under secure storage. We have and will continue to
refer all inquiries regarding the draft report to OSD for disposition.

4

MEMO FOR: MR. PETER NELSON

THROUGH: MR. MAYNARD ANDERSON

SUBJECT: PERSEREC Draft Report, Nonconforming Sexual Orientations

Thank you. I wanted to read the entire draft report, carefully and thoughtfully, and away from the heightened atmosphere of a few weeks back.

The basic work is fundamentally misdirected, as evidenced from the statement of objectives on page ii. Actually, the most explicit statement of our objective is indirectly set out in the sentence in the middle of page 22 which begins, "If there were a connection between being a homosexual and potential for security violation..." The existence or non-existence of that connection is precisely what we expected the analysis to address. This analysis would have presupposed that homosexuals were suitable for military service.

The study also wholly ignores the fact that a substantial part of our personnel security investigations involve persons in the private sector.

This entire effort, at least to date, is unfortunate.

- It has expended considerable government resources, and has not assisted us one whit in our personnel security program.

- It will be seized upon by critics of PERSEREC as evidence of the ineffective performance of that institution.

- It most probably will cause us in Washington to expend even more time and effort satisfying concerns in this whole issue area both in Congress and the media, and within the Department itself.

The actions we have directed recently may yield some usefulness yet; they will not, however, undo the above effects.

If it were not for all of the above, the situation could be humorous. It is as if <u>Consumers' Reports</u> commissioned research on the handling characteristics of the Suzuki Sammurai, and received instead a report arguing that informal import quotas for Japanese automobiles were not justified.

Craig Alderman, Jr.

cc:
Mr. Eoyang

[handwritten note: You might want to see my personal reactions to the Continental report —]

DATE RECEIVED

Part 3: The Second Report

**Preservice Adjustment of Homosexual and
Heterosexual Military Accessions:
Implications for Security Clearance Suitability**

Preservice Adjustment of Homosexual
and Heterosexual Military Accessions:
Implications for Security Clearance Suitability

Prepared by
Michael A. McDaniel

Reviewed by
Carson Eoyang
Director

Defense Personnel Security Research and Education Center
Monterey, California 93940-2481

Preface

The differences between homosexuals and others in society have long been subjects of great debate. More often than not, the controversy has suffered from a paucity of scientific research that could illuminate and inform the issues. This study is a limited effort to address the question: How do homosexuals differ from non-homosexuals in preservice adjustment characteristics? By exploring these differences, which may have direct security implications, this research helps increase our knowledge base pertaining to the suitability of homosexuals for positions of trust. This technical report is a revision of an earlier draft report entitled "The Suitability of Homosexuals for Positions of Trust" (November, 1987).

Carson K. Eoyang
Director

i

Preservice Adjustment of Homosexual
and Heterosexual Military Accessions:
Implications for Security Clearance Suitability

Prepared by
Michael A. McDaniel

Summary

Problem

Homosexuality is a topic of considerable debate and litigation in the national security community. The debate centers around the suitability of homosexuals for positions that require national security clearances.

Objective

The objective of the present study was to determine whether homosexuality is an indicator that a person possesses characteristics, separate from sexual orientation, that make one unsuitable for positions of trust. Specifically, this paper attempts to answer the question: How do homosexuals differ from heterosexuals in background characteristics relevant to security suitability?

Approach

To answer this question, background data were drawn from the Educational and Biographical Information Survey (EBIS) (Means & Perelman, 1984). This self-report inventory contains questions regarding educational experiences, drug and alcohol use, criminal activities, and driving record. Military accessions who were discharged from the service for homosexuality were compared with other military accessions on preservice background characteristics relevant to security suitability.

ii

Results

The data indicate that the suitability of homosexuals relative to heterosexuals depends upon the background area examined and the sex of the comparison group:

o   In general, homosexuals showed better preservice adjustment than heterosexuals in areas relating to school behavior.

o   Homosexuals also displayed greater levels of cognitive ability than heterosexuals.

o   Homosexuals, however, showed less preservice adjustment than heterosexuals in the area of drug and alcohol use.

o   With the exception of drug and alcohol use, homosexuals resemble those who successfully adjust to military life more so than those who are discharged for unsuitability.

o   Although male homosexuals tend to be better than or as equally adjusted as male heterosexuals with respect to the indices examined, female homosexuals' tend to score lower on preservice adjustment indices than female heterosexuals. However, females as a whole tended to show better preservice adjustment than males, and female homosexuals tended to have better preservice adjustment than most heterosexual male accessions.

Conclusion

The discussion section of this report lists several limitations of this study. Although these limitations should be carefully considered, the preponderance of the evidence presented in this study indicates that homosexuals show preservice suitability-related adjustment that is as good or better than the average heterosexual.

iii

Introduction

Homosexuality is a topic of considerable debate and litigation in the national security community (National Security Institute, 1987). Questions in the national security/homosexuality debate include:

1. Does the homosexuality of a security clearance holder present an exploitable vulnerability for hostile intelligence agencies?

2. Does the presence of a homosexual in a military or nonmilitary work group cause the group work performance or security climate to decay?

3. Is homosexuality an indicator that a potential security clearance holder possesses characteristics, separate from sexual orientation, that make one unsuitable for positions of trust?

This paper primarily addresses the third question. Specifically, this paper attempts to answer the question: How do homosexuals differ from heterosexuals in background characteristics relevant to security suitability? Thus, this paper has a narrow focus and does not address all questions concerning the suitability of homosexuals for employment in positions that require national security clearances.

A major problem in resolving the issue of the suitability of homosexuals for positions of trust is the paucity of research available on this topic. Recently, Ellis and Ames (1987) reviewed the literature on the origins of sexual orientation. After reviewing the literature on experiential, social-environmental, genetic, and physiological explanations of the causal determinants of sexual orientation, they concluded that the evidence best supports the position that sexual orientation is largely determined by genetic, neurological, hormonal, and environmental factors prior to birth. However, regardless of the origin of sexual orientation, there is little research addressing the suitability of homosexuals for positions of trust. This report is an attempt to address this research gap.

1

Approach

This study focuses on the question, "With reference to the types of background data normally collected in security-related background investigations, how do homosexuals and heterosexuals differ?" To answer this question, background data were drawn from the Educational and Biographical Information Survey (EBIS) (Means & Perelman, 1984). This self-report inventory contains questions regarding educational experiences, drug and alcohol use, criminal activities, and driving record. The EBIS data differ from most background investigation data, such as that collected by the Defense Investigative Service, in that the information was collected in a structured format (i.e., multiple choice questions), does not contain interview data or data from official sources such as police departments or credit agencies (i.e., all information was self reported), and contains more school adjustment questions than is obtained in most background investigations. However, the data set does tap the most common data domains in background investigations, and thus appears well suited for the present inquiry.

During the spring of 1983, the EBIS was administered to approximately 34,000 military applicants and 40,000 new recruits from all four services. The applicants who did not enter the military were categorized by gender. The military personnel were classified by gender, education, military career changes, and level of security clearance. Military discharge data on the EBIS respondents were obtained from the Defense Manpower Data Center. For this analysis, all military personnel who were discharged for homosexuality were separated from all other military accessions. The definition for all analysis groups in this study are:

Homosexuals:

Military personnel who were discharged for homosexuality. This group was further divided by gender.

Applicants Not Entering Service:

Military applicants who did not enter the military service. These persons took the EBIS as military applicants and either declined service entry or were refused admission. This group was divided by gender.

All Other Accessions:

All military accessions, except those discharged as homosexuals. Separate analyses were conducted by gender, education (high school diploma or not), military career changes, and level of security clearance. The categories of military career change were:

3

1) those discharged for unsuitability for reasons other than homosexuality,
2) those released from service,
3) those who sought immediate reenlistment in the military service,
4) those enlisted personnel who were granted entry into officer training programs,
5) those who received medical discharges, and
6) those who were still in the military, but who did not fit any of the above categories (these were labelled "not separated").

For the clearance level categorization, the military personnel were divided into those without a Secret or higher clearance (these were labelled "no clearance"), those with a Secret clearance, those with a Top Secret clearance but no SCI access, and those with a Top Secret clearance with SCI access or eligibility for SCI access.

Statistical methods were used to cluster the EBIS background data into meaningful clusters. The EBIS data formed seven clusters of background data that provided a useful summary of the recruits' preservice behavior. Six clusters are described below. The seventh background area, Grades and Socio-Economic Status, was not examined in this paper since it is not an area that is normally examined in security-related background investigations. For the remaining six categories, the items in each cluster were summed to yield six scale scores.

The scale contents were:

1. Major School Problems:

    Suspension from school, fighting in school, trouble in schools for being disorderly, using bad language, and smoking.

2. Drugs and Alcohol:

    Use of marijuana, stimulants, depressants, cocaine, heroin, other narcotics, other drugs, alcohol, cigarettes.

3. Job Experience:

    Reasons for leaving past jobs. Length of past full-time and part-time work.

4. Criminal Felonies:

    Adult and juvenile arrests and convictions.

5. Minor School Problems:

    Missing school, missing class, thoughts about quitting school.

4

6. Drunk & Disorderly:

Problems with alcohol, disorderly conduct, drunk driving, drug-related arrest, assault, misdemeanors.

The six background scales were standardized and expressed as percentiles. The higher the percentile for a group of persons the more favorable is the group's past life experience. The scales were standardized so that the average male military accessions are at the 50th percentile. Those groups with a percentile of greater than 50 had fewer preservice difficulties than the average male military accession. Those groups with a percentile of less than 50, on the average, had more preservice adjustment problems than the average male military accession. In each military group examined, there is considerable variability around each group's mean percentile. Thus, for example, if homosexuals are at the 45th percentile in a background domain, it means that on the average the homosexuals had more preservice adjustment problems than the male accessions. However, there will be substantial overlap in the distribution of the two groups such that some homosexuals will be more suitable than most of the male recruits.

In addition to the six background scales, the analysis groups were compared on Armed Forces Qualification Test (AFQT) percentiles. The AFQT is a measure of cognitive ability. The AFQT percentile reflects the scaling of the AFQT determined by DoD and was not normed so that all male accessions were at the 50th percentile.

In these analyses, the percentile standing of homosexuals on a given background scale is compared with the percentile standings of various other groups. In these comparisons, a difference of five percentile points was considered a meaningful difference. While this is a somewhat arbitrary decision rule, it appears to be a reasonable one. Those who wish to adopt a different decision rule may easily do so by examining the percentiles presented in the tables.

5

The six background scales appear to be relatively independent. The Major and Minor School Problems scales are the most similar item clusters. The Major School Problems scale appears to tap more serious problems in school, while the Minor School Problems scale is composed of less serious indicators of school adjustment.

The Drugs and Alcohol scale is distinguished from the Drunk and Disorderly scale in that the Drugs and Alcohol scale measures frequency of drug use, while the Drunk and Disorderly scale taps the amount of trouble one gets into as a result of drug and alcohol use. Both the Drunk and Disorderly scale and the Drugs and Alcohol scale have moderate correlations with all other scales. Since the six background scales were relatively distinct, it is most meaningful to compare the homosexuals and other groups on each of the six scales.

<u>Results for the Major School Problems Scale</u>

Table 1 displays the results for the background scale "Major School Problems:" This scale reflects serious school problems including suspension from school, fighting in school, trouble in school for being disorderly, using bad language, and smoking. Those with SCI clearances showed better adjustment than the Top Secret clearance holders without SCI access, who in turn showed better adjustment than the Secret clearance holders, who in turn showed better adjustment than those with no clearance. This monotonic relationship between level of adjustment and clearance level supports the hypothesis that the Major School Problems scale is a relevant background scale for accessing preservice adjustment.

In accordance with the 5-percentile definition of a meaningful difference, only differences of that magnitude or larger are noted. Given that male and female homosexuals showed meaningfully different levels of preservice adjustment in this area, they are discussed separately.

On the whole, the homosexuals showed better preservice adjustment on the Major School Problems scale than most other comparison groups. On the average, male homosexuals showed better preservice adjustment (59th percentile) on the Major School Problems scale than did the group of male military accessions (50th percentile). Male homosexuals on the average displayed substantially greater preservice adjustment on this dimension than the average heterosexual person discharged for unsuitability (40th percentile), and those without high school diplomas (32nd percentile). The male homosexuals had fewer major school problems than heterosexuals who were discharged for unsuitability, released from service, and who received medical discharges. Male homosexuals (59th percentile) also had better levels of preservice

7

Table 1

Major School Problems Background Scale.
Comparison of Homosexuals with Other Groups.
Higher Scores Indicate Better Adjustment.

Comparison Groups[1]	N	Percentile
Homosexuals	166	61
Males	113	59
Females	53	66
Applicants Not		
Entering Service[2]	16,357	56
Males	12,525	52
Females	3,720	71
All Other Accessions	48,302	53
Males	42,095	50
Females	6,207	73
High School Graduate	43,233	56
GED and Nongraduates	5,069	32
Military Career Changes[3]		
Unsuitability Discharges	8,468	40
Release From Service	6,855	53
Immediate Reenlistment	4,023	57
Officer	277	75
Medical	1,838	49
Not Separated	24,970	57
Clearance Category		
No Clearance	27,347	50
Secret	18,181	56
Top Secret (no SCI)	1,152	64
SCI	1,622	68

[1]Homosexuals were defined as those released from military service for homosexuality. Applicants not entering service were those military applicants who completed the EBIS but did not join the service.

[2]The gender of 112 military applicants who did not enter service is unknown.

[3]A total of 1,871 persons had military career changes which are not one of those in the table.

8

adjustment than those without clearances (50th percentile), and showed no meaningful difference in preservice adjustment from those holding Secret clearances. Male homosexuals, however, showed meaningfully less preservice adjustment on the Major School Problems dimension than enlisted personnel who entered officer training, and Top Secret and SCI clearance holders.

Regardless of sexual orientation, females showed better levels of preservice adjustment on Major School Problems scale than males. Female accessions were at the 73rd percentile, while female applicants not entering the service were at the 71st percentile. However, in contrast to the male homosexuals who had fewer preservice adjustment problems in this area than the average male accession, female homosexuals had more preservice adjustment problems than the average female accession (66th percentile vs. 73rd percentile). Although female homosexuals showed poorer preservice adjustment on the Major School Problems scale than heterosexual females, the homosexual females showed better adjustment than most other comparison groups including those with Top Secret and SCI clearances.

Results for the Drug and Alcohol Scale

Table 2 displays the results for the background scale "Drugs and Alcohol." This scale primarily measures admissions concerning the quantity of drugs and alcohol consumed by the respondent. The higher the clearance level the greater the preservice adjustment on the drug and alcohol scale. This monotonic relationship between level of adjustment and clearance level supports the belief that the Drug and Alcohol scale is a relevant background scale for accessing preservice adjustment.

In contrast to the Major School Problems scale, homosexuals showed worse preservice adjustment on the Drugs and Alcohol scale than most other comparison groups. The difference between male and female homosexuals on the Drugs and Alcohol scale was small (43rd vs. 45th percentile). The homosexuals appear to use about as much drugs and alcohol as the non-high school graduates (41st percentile) and the unsuitability discharges (43rd percentile).

Homosexuals showed meaningfully less preservice adjustment on the Drugs and Alcohol dimension than all male accessions, all female accessions, high school graduates, those released from the service, those who sought immediate reenlistment, those who entered officer training, medical discharges, and those who did not separate. All levels of clearance holders showed better levels of preservice adjustment on the Drugs and Alcohol scale than did the homosexuals.

9

Table 2

Drugs and Alcohol Background Scale.
Comparison of Homosexuals with Other Groups.
Higher Scores Indicate Better Adjustment.

Comparison Groups[1]	N	Percentile
Homosexuals	166	44
Males	113	43
Females	53	45
Applicants Not		
Entering Service[2]	16,357	58
Males	12,525	55
Females	3,720	64
All Other Accessions	48,302	51
Males	42,095	50
Females	6,207	58
High School Graduate	43,233	52
GED and Nongraduates	5,069	41
Military Career Changes[3]		
Unsuitability Discharges	8,468	43
Release From Service	6,855	51
Immediate Reenlistment	4,023	57
Officer	277	58
Medical	1,838	51
Not Separated	24,970	53
Clearance Category		
No Clearance	27,347	50
Secret	18,181	52
Top Secret (no SCI)	1,152	53
SCI	1,622	57

---

[1]Homosexuals were defined as those released from military service for homosexuality.
Applicants not entering service were those military applicants who completed the EBIS but did not join the service.
[2]The gender of 112 military applicants who did not enter service is unknown.
[3]A total of 1,871 persons had military career changes which are not one of those in the table.

10

Results for the Employment Experience Scale

Table 3 displays the results for the background scale "Employment Experience." This scale primarily measures the amount of one's job experience and the conditions under which one terminated employment. The level of preservice adjustment on this scale does not monotonically covary across clearance levels. This suggests that this scale may have less relevance for security suitability than other scales.

Whereas male homosexuals showed a meaningfully lower level of preservice adjustment on the Employment Experience scale than female homosexuals, the two homosexuals groups are discussed separately.

The male homosexuals showed less preservice adjustment on this scale (48th percentile) than those who sought immediate reenlistment and those who did not separate. Male homosexuals were not, however, meaningfully different from any of the groups holding security clearances. In general, there was little differentiation in employment experience adjustment among any of the comparison groups. This was probably due to the limited amount of job experience for those who enter the military.

Female homosexuals (58th percentile) showed the same level of preservice adjustment on the employment experience scale as heterosexual females. Females, regardless of their sexual orientation, showed better levels of preservice adjustment on this scale than most other comparison groups, including those with Secret clearances, Top Secret clearances and those with SCI access.

Results for the Felonies Scale

Table 4 displays the results for the background scale "Felonies." This scale measures the number of felony arrests and convictions. Those with SCI clearances showed better adjustment than the Top Secret clearance holders without SCI access, who in turn showed better adjustment than the Secret clearance holders, who in turn showed better adjustment than those with no clearance. This monotonic relationship between level of adjustment and clearance level supports the hypothesis that the Felonies scale is a relevant background scale for accessing preservice adjustment.

Since male homosexuals showed meaningfully lower levels of preservice adjustment than female homosexuals on the Felonies scale, the comparison is discussed separately.

11

Table 3

Employment Experience Background Scale.
Comparison of Homosexuals with Other Groups.
Higher Scores Indicate Better Adjustment.

Comparison Groups[1]	N	Percentile
Homosexuals	166	51
Males	113	48
Females	53	58
Applicants Not		
Entering Service[2]	16,357	59
Males	12,525	56
Females	3,720	66
All Other Accessions	48,302	51
Males	42,095	50
Females	6,207	58
High School Graduate	43,233	52
GED and Nongraduates	5,069	46
Military Career Changes[3]		
Unsuitability Discharges	8,468	46
Release From Service	6,855	52
Immediate Reenlistment	4,023	53
Officer	277	50
Medical	1,838	44
Not Separated	24,970	53
Clearance Category		
No Clearance	27,347	51
Secret	18,181	51
Top Secret (no SCI)	1,152	49
SCI	1,622	52

---

[1]Homosexuals were defined as those released from military service for homosexuality.
Applicants not entering service were those military applicants who completed the EBIS but did not join the service.
[2]The gender of 112 military applicants who did not enter service is unknown.
[3]A total of 1,871 persons had military career changes which are not one of those in the table.

12

Table 4

Felonies Background Scale.
Comparison of Homosexuals with Other Groups.
Higher Scores Indicate Better Adjustment.

Comparison Groups[1]	N	Percentile
Homosexuals	166	51
Males	113	47
Females	53	59
Applicants Not		
Entering Service[2]	16,357	48
Males	12,525	46
Females	3,720	58
All Other Accessions	48,302	51
Males	42,095	50
Females	6,207	59
High School Graduate	43,233	52
GED and Nongraduates	5,069	44
Military Career Changes[3]		
Unsuitability Discharges	8,468	46
Release From Service	6,855	51
Immediate Reenlistment	4,023	52
Officer	277	56
Medical	1,838	50
Not Separated	24,970	52
Clearance Category		
No Clearance	27,347	49
Secret	18,181	53
Top Secret (no SCI)	1,152	57
SCI	1,622	58

---

[1]Homosexuals were defined as those released from military service for homosexuality.
Applicants not entering service were those military applicants who completed the EBIS but did not join the service.
[2]The gender of 112 military applicants who did not enter service is unknown.
[3]A total of 1,871 persons had military career changes which are not one of those in the table.

13

Male homosexuals (47th percentile) showed worse preservice adjustment than high school graduates, those who obtained immediate reenlistment, those who entered officer training, and those who did not separate. Male homosexuals also showed lower levels of preservice adjustment than those who held clearances.

In contrast to the male homosexuals, female homosexuals had better levels of adjustment on the Felonies dimension than most comparison groups. Female homosexuals showed better adjustment on the Felonies scale than high school graduates, non-high school graduates, unsuitability discharges, those released from service, those who received immediate reenlistment, medical discharges, those not separated, and those with Secret clearances. There was no meaningful difference in preservice adjustment on the Felonies dimension between female homosexuals and Top Secret and SCI clearance holders.

Results for the Minor School Problems Scale

Table 5 displays the results for the Minor School Problems background scale. This scale measures minor school problems such as missing class and thoughts about quitting school. The higher the clearance level the greater the preservice adjustment on the Minor School Problems scale. This monotonic relationship between level of adjustment and clearance level supports the contention that the Minor School Problems scale is a relevant background scale for accessing preservice adjustment.

Because male homosexuals showed lower preservice adjustment on this dimension than female homosexuals, the comparisons are discussed separately.

Male homosexuals (52nd percentile) showed little difference from most comparison groups including those with Secret clearances. Homosexuals had lower levels of preservice adjustment than high school graduates, those who entered officer training, and Top Secret (nonSCI) and SCI clearance holders. Male homosexuals had higher levels of preservice adjustment on the Minor School Problems dimension than non-high school graduates, heterosexual unsuitability discharges, and medical discharges.

Females, regardless of sexual orientation, showed higher levels of preservice adjustment on the Minor School Problems scale than most other comparison groups, with female homosexuals (58th percentile) showing less preservice adjustment than female accessions (63rd percentile). Female homosexuals had fewer preservice adjustment problems in this area than non-high school graduates, unsuitability discharges, those released from service, medical discharges, and those without clearances.

14

Table 5

Minor School Problems Background Scale.
Comparison of Homosexuals with Other Groups.
Higher Scores Indicate Better Adjustment.

Comparison Groups[1]	N	Percentile
Homosexuals	166	54
Males	113	52
Females	53	58
Applicants Not Entering Service[2]	16,357	50
Males	12,525	47
Females	3,720	61
All Other Accessions	48,302	52
Males	42,095	50
Females	6,207	63
High School Graduate	43,233	59
GED and Nongraduates	5,069	9
Military Career Changes[3]		
Unsuitability Discharges	8,468	37
Release From Service	6,855	51
Immediate Reenlistment	4,023	55
Officer	277	89
Medical	1,838	47
Not Separated	24,970	56
Clearance Category		
No Clearance	27,347	48
Secret	18,181	55
Top Secret (no SCI)	1,152	64
SCI	1,622	68

---

[1]Homosexuals were defined as those released from military service for homosexuality. Applicants not entering service were those military applicants who completed the EBIS but did not join the service.

[2]The gender of 112 military applicants who did not enter service is unknown.

[3]A total of 1,871 persons had military career changes which are not one of those in the table.

15

GAYS IN UNIFORM

Results for the Drunk and Disorderly Scale

Table 6 displays the results for the Drunk and Disorderly scale. This scale includes items regarding drunk driving arrests, drug-related arrests, and misdemeanors. Those with SCI clearances showed better adjustment than the Top Secret clearance holders without SCI access, who in turn showed better adjustment than the Secret clearance holders, who in turn showed better adjustment than those with no clearance. This relationship between level of adjustment and clearance level supports the contention that the Drunk and Disorderly scale is a relevant background scale for accessing preservice adjustment.

Male and female homosexuals showed approximately equal levels of preservice adjustment on this scale. When homosexuals showed meaningful differences with other comparison groups, the differences typically indicated that the homosexuals had higher levels of preservice adjustment.

Results for the AFQT Percentile

Table 7 presents the results for the AFQT analyses. The AFQT can be viewed as a measure of general cognitive ability. The AFQT has a DoD-dictated norming standard which was used in this analysis. Consequently, the male accession percentile is not 50. The higher the clearance level, the greater the average AFQT percentile. Although cognitive ability is not a topic explored in the typical background investigation, this monotonic relationship between AFQT and clearance level supports the contention that the AFQT Percentile is a relevant background characteristic for accessing preservice adjustment.

Male and female homosexuals showed similar levels of AFQT scores which tend to be higher than those for other comparison groups. Female homosexuals showed greater cognitive ability than unsuitability discharges, those released from service, those who received immediate reenlistment, and medical discharges. Male homosexuals showed greater cognitive ability than all these groups and also showed greater cognitive ability than male and female accessions, accessions regardless of educational status, and Secret clearance holders. Those enlisted personnel who entered officer training and SCI clearance holders, however, showed greater levels of cognitive ability than homosexuals.

16

Table 6

Drunk and Disorderly Background Scale.
Comparison of Homosexuals with Other Groups.
Higher Scores Indicate Better Adjustment.

Comparison Groups[1]	N	Percentile
Homosexuals	166	56
Males	113	56
Females	53	55
Applicants Not		
Entering Service[2]	16,357	51
Males	12,525	48
Females	3,720	63
All Other Accessions	48,302	52
Males	42,095	50
Females	6,207	62
High School Graduate	43,233	53
GED and Nongraduates	5,069	45
Military Career Changes[3]		
Unsuitability Discharges	8,468	46
Release From Service	6,855	50
Immediate Reenlistment	4,023	55
Officer	277	59
Medical	I,838	52
Not Separated	24,970	53
Clearance Category		
No Clearance	27,347	49
Secret	18,181	55
Top Secret (no SCI)	1,152	58
SCI	1,622	61

---

[1]Homosexuals were defined as those released from military service for homosexuality.
Applicants not entering service were those military applicants who completed the EBIS but did not join the service.

[2]The gender of 112 military applicants who did not enter service is unknown.

[3]A total of 1,871 persons had military career changes which are not one of those in the table.

17

Table 7

AFQT Percentile.
Comparison of Homosexuals with Other Groups.
Higher Scores Indicate Higher Ability.

Comparison Groups[1]	N	Percentile
Homosexuals	164	63
Males	111	64
Females	53	62
Applicants Not Entering Service[2]	---	---
Males	---	---
Females	---	---
All Other Accessions	48,055	58
Males	41,863	58
Females	6,192	60
High School Graduate	43,028	58
GED and Nongraduates	5,027	58
Military Career Changes[3]		
Unsuitability Discharges	8,441	55
Release From Service	6,708	53
Immediate Reenlistment	4,022	54
Officer	273	85
Medical	l,833	56
Not Separated	24,917	61
Clearance Category		
No Clearance	27,173	56
Secret	18,122	59
Top Secret (no SCI)	1,144	66
SCI	1,616	72

---

[1]Homosexuals were defined as those released from military service for homosexuality.
[2]AFQT data for applicants not entering service were not available.
[3]A total of 1,861 persons had military career changes which are not one of those in the table.

18

Discussion

This study indicates that the suitability of homosexuals relative to heterosexuals depends upon the preservice background area examined and the sex of the comparison group. In general, homosexuals showed better preservice adjustment than heterosexuals in areas relating to school behavior. Homosexuals also showed greater levels of cognitive ability than heterosexuals. Homosexuals, however, showed less adjustment than heterosexuals in the area of drug and alcohol use. Male homosexuals also showed less adjustment than several comparison groups on the Felonies scale. Except for preservice drug and alcohol use (and homosexual males adjustment on the Felonies scale), homosexuals more closely resemble those who successfully adjust to military life than those who are discharged for unsuitability. While male homosexuals appeared to have better or equal preservice adjustment patterns than male heterosexuals, female homosexuals tended to have somewhat poorer preservice adjustment patterns than female heterosexuals. However, females as a whole tended to show higher levels of preservice adjustment than males, and female homosexuals tended to have higher levels of preservice adjustment than most heterosexual male accessions.

One may question the appropriateness of the background scales used in this analysis. It could be argued that one or more of these background areas are irrelevant to suitability for positions of trust. For example, the Defense Investigative Service no longer devotes extensive investigative resources to collecting school-related background information. Two lines of evidence, however, support the relevance of these background areas for employment suitability. First, with the possible exception of the school adjustment clusters, the background areas have similar content to those used by DoD background investigators. Second, the results for these background scales showed a meaningful pattern of relationships across comparison groups. Those enlisted personnel who entered officer training had higher levels of preservice adjustment than other successful accessions who had higher levels of preservice adjustment than heterosexuals discharged for unsuitability. Except for the Employment Experience scale, those with SCI access had higher levels of preservice adjustment than those with non-SCI Top Secret clearances, who had fewer preservice adjustment problems than Secret clearance holders, who had higher levels of preservice adjustment than those who did not have a Secret or higher clearance.

Limitations of the Present Study

While this report makes a significant contribution to understanding homosexual suitability for positions of trust, the study suffers from several limitations. Five caveats are offered:

19

o   First, the paper has a limited focus. It does not address the issue of homosexuality as a vulnerability that may be exploitable by hostile intelligence agencies. Nor does it address the consequences of mixing homosexual and heterosexual persons in the same work group.

o   Second, the definitions used in this study for homosexual and heterosexual are not perfect. Some of those who received discharges for homosexuality may be heterosexuals who falsely professed to homosexuality to gain a prompt release from military service. Also, it is very likely that some members of the heterosexual group examined in this analysis were homosexuals. Only those homosexuals who were discharged from the military service for homosexuality were counted as homosexuals for this analysis. In addition, the homosexuality/heterosexuality dichotomy used in this study is an arbitrary one. Many people are neither exclusively homosexual nor exclusively heterosexual.

o   Third, homosexuals who choose to join the military may be very different from the population of young adult homosexuals who are potential military accessions and may be very different from civilian homosexuals who seek national security clearances.

o   Fourth, the calculation of the percentiles presented in the tables implicitly assumes that the background scales scores are normally distributed. All of the background scales showed at least some departures from a normal distribution.

o   Fifth, relative to all other comparison groups in this analysis (viz., 42,095 male military accessions), the number of homosexuals was small (113 males and 53 females). Less confidence should be placed in conclusions drawn from smaller samples. Data collected on another group of homosexuals and heterosexuals will likely be somewhat different from the results in this study solely due to random sampling error.

20

Conclusion

In summary, this report has provided limited but cogent evidence regarding the preservice suitability of homosexuals who may apply for positions of trust. Although this study has several limitations, the preponderance of the evidence presented indicates that homosexuals show preservice suitability-related adjustment that is as good or better than the average heterosexual. Thus, these results appear to be in conflict with conceptions of homosexuals as unstable, maladjusted persons. Given the critical importance of appropriate policy in the national security area, additional research attention to this area is warranted.

21

References

Ellis, L., & Ames, M. A. (1987). Neurohormonal functioning and sexual orientation: A theory of homosexuality-heterosexuality. Psychological Bulletin, 101, 233-258.

Means, B., & Perelman, L. S. (1984). The development of the Educational and Background Information Survey. FR-PRD-84-3. Alexandria, VA: Human Resources Research Organization.

National Security Institute (1987). Court rules for gays. NSI Advisory, 3, 4.

23

Other books of interest from
ALYSON PUBLICATIONS

TORN ALLEGIANCES, by Jim Holobaugh, with Keith Hale, $10.00. Jim Holobaugh was the perfect ROTC cadet — so perfect that ROTC featured the handsome college student in a nationwide ad campaign. But as he gradually came to realize that he was gay, he faced an impossible dilemma: To serve the country he loved, he would have to live a life of deceit. His story dramatizes both the monetary waste, and the moral corruptness, of the military's anti-gay policy.

MATLOVICH, by Mike Hippler, $9.00. Air Force Sergeant Leonard Matlovich appeared on the cover of *Time* magazine when he was discharged for being gay — and decided to fight back. This courageous activist did not fit the usual gay stereotype, and his outspoken, generally conservative views created controversy over his role as a community leader. Mike Hippler has written, with Matlovich's cooperation, the definitive biography of this gay hero.

SOCIETY AND THE HEALTHY HOMOSEXUAL, by George Weinberg; introduction by Gerry E. Studds, $8.00. Rarely has anyone communicated so much, in a single word, as Dr. George Weinberg did when he introduced the term *homophobia* to a wide audience. With a single stroke of the pen, he turned the tables on centuries of prejudice. Homosexuality is healthy, said Weinberg: homophobia is a sickness. In this pioneering book, Weinberg examines the causes of homophobia. He shows how gay people can overcome its pervasive influence, to lead happy and fulfilling lives.

KEYS TO CARING, edited by Robert J. Kus, $13.00. Thirty-one essays offer informed advice to health care and other professionals about how to better serve gay and lesbian clients. Dr. Kus, a nurse-sociologist and professor, has selected essays by gay people who are experts in a variety of health-care-related fields. Topics explored include homophobia, body image, parenting, AIDS, coming out, spirituality, and legal issues.

ONE TEENAGER IN TEN, edited by Ann Heron, $5.00. One teenager in ten is gay. Here, twenty-six young people from around the country discuss their experiences: coming out to themselves, to parents, and friends; trying to pass as straight; running away; incest; trouble with the law; making initial contacts with the gay community; religious concerns; and more. Their words will provide encouragement for other teenagers facing similar experiences.

THE MEN WITH THE PINK TRIANGLE, by Heinz Heger, $8.00. For decades, history ignored the Nazi persecution of gay people. Only with the rise of the gay movement in the 1970s did historians finally recognize that gay people, like Jews and others deemed "undesirable," suffered enormously at the hands of the Nazi regime. Of the few who survived the concentration camps, only one ever came forward to tell his story. His true account of those nightmarish years provides an important introduction to a long-forgotten chapter of gay history.

THE TROUBLE WITH HARRY HAY, by Stuart Timmons, $13.00. This complete biography of Harry Hay, known as the father of gay liberation, sweeps through forty years of the gay movement and nearly eighty years of a colorful and original American life. Hay went from a pampered childhood, through a Hollywood acting career and a stint in the Communist Party before starting his life's work in 1950 when he founded the Mattachine Society, the forerunner of today's gay movement.

BI ANY OTHER NAME, edited by Loraine Hutchins and Lani Kaahumanu, $12.00. Hear the voices of over seventy women and men from all walks of life describe their lives as bisexuals. They tell their stories — personal, political, spiritual, historical — in prose, poetry, art, and essays. These are individuals who have fought prejudice from both the gay and straight communities and who have begun only recently to share their experiences. This ground-breaking anthology is an important step in the process of forming a new bisexual community.

BROTHER TO BROTHER, edited by Essex Hemphill, $9.00. Black activist and poet Essex Hemphill has carried on in the footsteps of the late Joseph Beam (editor of *In the Life*) with this new anthology of fiction, essays, and poetry by black gay men. Contributors include Assoto Saint, Craig G. Harris, Melvin Dixon, Marlon Riggs, and many newer writers.

BETTER ANGEL, by Richard Meeker, $7.00. The touching story of a young man's gay awakening in the years between the World Wars. Kurt Gray is a shy, bookish boy growing up in a small town in Michigan. Even at the age of thirteen he knows that somehow he is different. Gradually he recognizes his desire for a man's companionship and love. As a talented composer, breaking into New York's musical world, he finds the love he's sought.

HIV-POSITIVE: WORKING THE SYSTEM, by Robert A. Rimer and Michael A. Connolly, $13.00. Nobody — including your doctor — cares as much about keeping you alive as you do. That's the fundamental message of this innovative, humorous, and immensely useful guide for anyone who is HIV-positive. Don't leave the decisions up to your doctor, the authors advise. Make sure that *you* understand what your options are, and what the consequences are likely to be. Your life depends on it.

GAY MEN AND WOMEN WHO ENRICHED THE WORLD, by Thomas Cowan, $9.00. Growing up gay in a straight culture, writes Thomas Cowan, challenges the individual in special ways. Here are lively accounts of forty personalities who have offered outstanding contributions in fields ranging from mathematics and military strategy to art, philosophy, and economics. Each chapter is amusingly illustrated with a caricature by Michael Willhoite.

GOLDENBOY, by Michael Nava, $9.00. Jim Pears is guilty; even his lawyer, Henry Rios, believes that. The evidence is overwhelming that Pears killed the co-worker who threatened to expose his homosexuality. But as Rios investigates the case, he finds that the pieces don't always fit together the way they should. Too many people *want* Jim Pears to be found guilty, regardless of the truth. And some of them are determined that Henry Rios isn't going to interfere with their plans.

TREASURES ON EARTH, by Carter Wilson, $9.00. First published in cloth by Knopf in 1981, *Treasures on Earth* tells the "shadow history" of the historic 1911 expedition that led to the discovery of Machu Picchu in the Peruvian Andes. While the explorers search greedily for the "lost" city and the acclaim that will certainly follow, Willie Hickler, the expedition's photographer (and Wilson's central and fictional character), searches for love with Ernesto Mena, the expedition's handsome Peruvian guide.

EIGHT DAYS A WEEK, by Larry Duplechan, $7.00. Johnnie Ray Rousseau is a 22-year-old black gay pop singer whose day starts at 11 p.m. Keith Keller is a white banker with a 10 o'clock bedtime — and muscles to die for. This story of their love affair is one of the most engrossing — and funniest — you'll ever read.

OUT OF ALL TIME, by Terry Boughner, $7.00. Historian Terry Boughner scans the centuries and picks out scores of the past's most celebrated gay, lesbian, and bisexual personalities. From ancient Egypt to the twentieth century, from Alcibiades to Willa Cather, we discover a part of history that has too often been censored or ignored. Each chapter is imaginatively illustrated by *Washington Blade* caricaturist Michael Willhoite.

THE GAY BOOK OF LISTS, by Leigh Rutledge, $9.00. Rutledge has compiled a fascinating and informative collection of lists. His subject matter ranges from history (6 gay popes) to politics (9 perfectly disgusting reactions to AIDS) to entertainment (12 examples of gays on network television) to humor (9 Victorian "cures" for masturbation). Learning about gay culture and history has never been so much fun.

THE ALYSON ALMANAC, by Alyson Publications, $9.00. How did your representatives in Congress vote on gay issues? What are the best gay and lesbian books, movies, and plays? When was the first gay and lesbian march on Washington? With what king did Julius Caesar have a sexual relationship? You'll find all this, and more, in this unique and entertaining reference work.

Ask for these titles in your favorite bookstore. Or, to order by mail, use this coupon or a photocopy.

— — — — — — — — — — — —

Enclosed is $_____ for the following books. (Add $1.00 postage when ordering just one book. If you order two or more, we'll pay the postage.)

1. _____

2. _____

3. _____

4. _____

name: _____

address: _____

city: _____ state: _____ zip: _____

ALYSON PUBLICATIONS
Dept. H-81, 40 Plympton St., Boston, MA 02118

After Dec. 31, 1994, please write for current catalog.